Goronwy and Me

Goronwy and Me

A Narrative of Two Lives

PROAL HEARTWELL

RESOURCE *Publications* • Eugene, Oregon

GORONWY AND ME
A Narrative of Two Lives

Copyright © 2012 Proal Heartwell. All rights reserved. Except for brief quotations in critical publications or reviews, no part of this book may be reproduced in any manner without prior written permission from the publisher. Write: Permissions, Wipf and Stock Publishers, 199 W. 8th Ave., Suite 3, Eugene, OR 97401.

Resource Publications
An Imprint of Wipf and Stock Publishers
199 W. 8th Ave., Suite 3
Eugene, OR 97401

www.wipfandstock.com

ISBN 13: 978-1-62032-307-6

Manufactured in the U.S.A.

All quotations from *Goronwy Owen* by Branwen Jarvis reprinted with kind permission from the University of Wales Press.

Frontispiece illustration by Josef Beery

This book is dedicated to
Mother, for her wisdom and inspiration;
Susie and Elise, for their love and support;
the girls of Village School, past and present, for their curiosity and enthusiasm.

Y lle bum yn gwarae gynt
Mae dynion na'm hadwaenyt.
Cywydd Hiraeth Am Fon, by Goronwy Owen (II 11–12)

(In the place where I once played
Now there are men who know me not.)

Contents

Acknowledgments | ix

Part I: Goronwy Ddu O Fon (Goronwy the Black of Anglesea)
1 I Meet Goronwy Owen | 3
2 I Meet Goronwy Again | 10
3 Who Is Goronwy Owen | 18
4 Goronwy Considered | 32
5 Goronwy Celebrated | 48

Part II: Goronwy'R Alltud (Goronwy the Exile)
6 July, 1761 | 65
7 November, 1763 | 76
8 July, 1767 | 93
9 June/July, 1769 | 108

Part III: Bro Goronwy (The Land of Goronwy)
10 Môn | 121
11 Cymru | 133
12 Hiraeth | 143

Bibliography | 153

Acknowledgments

I AM INDEBTED TO many people for their help and encouragement in the writing of this book, including my siblings for their shared memories and steadfast support. The members of my writing group are to be commended for their patience and insightful reading. Thank you to Roderic Owen who first educated me to the vagaries of Welsh language and culture, and to Robert Jeffrey for his encyclopedic knowledge of all things Welsh and for his unflagging encouragement. I'm grateful to Randy Crenshaw for riding shotgun and to all the librarians who helped me in my quest to get to know Goronwy. In Wales, Dewi and Magdalen Jones, as well as Elizabeth Hughes, took a keen interest in my research and clearly articulated their affection for the exiled bard. Thanks also to the Brunswick County Museum and Historical Society (especially Magen Cywink) for giving me a forum to share my story. I'm grateful, too, for the technical help of Meredith Gould and to Christian Amondson of Wipf and Stock Publishers for shepherding me through unchartered territory. Finally, a heartfelt "thank you" to Laura Roseberry for her tireless effort and vision in support of this narrative.

PART I

Goronwy Ddu o Fon
(Goronwy the Black of Anglesea)

PART I

Coronus: The Sun God
or
(Gorbywog and Dick of America)

1

I Meet Goronwy Owen

NIGHT MUSIC
by Proal Heartwell

At twilight, we gather,
fresh from meals of silver-queen corn
and home-grown tomatoes.
James, the littlest, is "it,"
and he scurries after the can I kick
across the cobblestone walk to the privet hedge.
Our way lit by fireflies, we run to hide.
I crouch in the boxwood; Bill clambers up the maple
as only he can.
Sue, bereft of imagination, squats behind the porch rocker.
On and on we play, till stars appear
in the purple sky
and screams of "I see you" compete with
a choir of crickets.
Screen doors squeak open across the darkness;
mothers call, adding syllables to our names.
We run to our houses, wash behind our ears,
and climb under cool sheets.

Goronwy and Me

Alone in my bed, the film of my day reels by my eyes,
and a sudden breeze blows across my sun-tanned skin.
I reach for my grandmother's quilt, pull it to my chin,
and smell the memories hidden in
the strips of brightly colored fabric.
Slowly, peacefully, I fall into sleep.

I Meet Goronwy Owen

I WAKE UP EARLY in the quiet that is Sunday morning and walk down the squeaky stairs to the cold kitchen at the back of the house. I hastily pour my bowl of Cheerios, orange juice, and retreat to the family room and turn on the television. Adjusting the antenna, I plop to the floor, and watch Notre Dame football highlights with Lindsay Nelson, and try not to spill milk on Mother's carpet as I follow the weekly exploits of quarterback Terry Hanratty and the Fighting Irish.

All is quiet upstairs. Mother and Daddy sleep in after another late Saturday night at the country club, drinking Jack Daniel's old fashioneds and dancing to records by Keely Smith, Al Martino, and Peggy Lee. The older of my two sisters is gone and living in Richmond, having married this past July in what surely was the hottest wedding ever at St. Andrew's Episcopal Church. I was the acolyte at their celebration with an unimpeded view of the happy couple's sweat-glistened faces as they knelt to receive Dr. Tayloe's blessing.

My brother is away at college, and I sometimes sleep in his old bedroom and revel in its many mysteries: the Fairport Convention albums, the Lawrence Ferlinghetti books of poetry, the Eugene McCarthy for President poster on his wall. On this desk are pictures of his girlfriend, snapshots of their summer working at Virginia Beach. His Woodberry Forest yearbook, the *Fir Tree*, lies unopened nearby. In it, I know, is his photograph catching a touchdown pass against St. Christopher's. Will I, I often wonder, play football, too, when I go to Woodberry next year?

My older sister is still asleep and my parents will rouse her in a couple of hours to accompany them to church. She will begrudgingly acquiesce, weary from last night's date with Ronnie. They again have been forced to babysit me, which means they sit on the sofa, smoke cigarettes, drink Cokes, hold hands, and express annoyance at my presence. In time, I tire of their mutual self-absorption and head off to bed, where I read *The Mickey Mantle Story* for what must be the hundredth time.

Now, I turn off the TV and take my empty bowl and glass to the kitchen sink. I retreat to my room, dress, and outside my door, pick up the shoes my father polished for me before he went to bed last night. In the downstairs bathroom, I brush my teeth, attempt in vain to tame my cowlick hair, and put on my shoes.

I head out of the still slumbering house, careful to not let the screen door slam, and turn left down Windsor Avenue, toward St. Andrew's. The morning air is cool, but I have eschewed a jacket knowing the October sun will soon warm me. I walk past my grandmother's house, her Country Squire wagon in the driveway. The crape myrtle in the side yard still harbors a few rose-colored blossoms. Soon Granny will be up, fix her customary fried egg and Taylor's Ham, and begin the ritual of preparing for church. Fashionably attired, she will drive the two hundred yards to church, arriving five minutes after the service begins to join my family in "our" pew. After church, we will retire to Granny's house for sweet sugar mints, dry roasted peanuts, one glass of sherry each, and of course, her commentary on the dresses of the ladies of the congregation.

Across the street from Granny's house is the home of Miss Elfie and Miss Maude, spinster sisters who teach at the town elementary school. These no-nonsense ladies taught not only multiplication, long division, and sentence diagramming to me and my siblings, but to my father as well, who still quickly extinguishes his cigarette whenever he glimpses one of these arbiters of knowledge.

I walk past the home of my friend Joe, two years my elder and the other acolyte at our church, and I wonder if he has somehow sequestered the new *Playboy* in the small patch of woods behind his house. I know for ten cents, the cost of a Pepsi, Joe will let me gaze upon the magazine, and he will provide commentary beyond my wildest imagining.

On my left are the gates of St. Paul's College, an all black teacher training school supported by the Diocese of Southern Virginia. St. Paul's six hundred students rarely stray beyond the campus gates, and its faculty and staff seem known to only a few of the town's merchants, like my father, who is also Chair of the college's Board of Trustees. My interactions with the college are few: attending the occasional football game with my father, our faces conspicuous in a sea of brownish hues, or playing tennis in the summer with Joe on the college's (and the town's) lone court. I remember the disquietude I felt the previous fall when two professors from St. Paul's appeared in the narthex of our church at the beginning of the Sunday service. As they scanned the pews for a place to sit, my father quickly approached them, and after a hushed, seemingly cordial conversation, they left. Daddy returned to his seat and no mention of the encounter was made, then or later.

Now, as I walk towards the church, I again consider its well-worn, but welcoming visage. It's a modest structure of once-white clapboard siding and a gray slate roof. Over the bright red front door is a small round window where bubbled glass admits irregular shafts of light into the narthex.

I Meet Goronwy Owen

A bell tower is anchored to the rear of the building, looking like a turret transposed from another time and place. Built in 1829, the church is the oldest building in Lawrenceville, the parish having existed since 1732.

I enter the back door of the structure and glance about for C.P., my grandfather's half-brother, a retired bookkeeper who serves as the St. Andrew's Superintendent of Sunday School. We exchange brief pleasantries, and I set about my ritual tasks, first mounting on the board affixed to the transept wall near the pulpit, the day's designation in the liturgical calendar, and below that, the numbers of the service hymns. I weave through the ten rows of pews, intersected by a center aisle, placing the kneeling benches upright and confirming that each pew rack has a hymn book and the 1928 Book of Common Prayer with its arcane, yet resonant language. Soft morning light filters through the six stained glass windows, and smears of red, blue, and green rest on the pews' dark velvet cushions. I pause to read again the plaque mounted on the back wall, noting the four chandeliers given in memory of my grandfather. These brass fixtures are suspended over the nave and cast a diffuse soft glow throughout the worship space.

I retrieve the thin wafers and Mogen David wine from the small sacristy and fill the chalice and cruet on the table next to the altar, believing, I suppose, that through Dr. Tayloe's intercession, these elements will shortly be transfigured into the body and blood of Christ. It is now ten thirty, and I don my well-worn acolyte robes and receive last minute, but familiar instructions from Dr. Tayloe, "Doc" as he is known to the adults of the parish. Mindful that I am to be confirmed in the spring, he asks if I have memorized the Ten Commandments and the Apostles' Creed. I answer in the affirmative, and, at precisely 10:45, I ring the bell to summon the morning worshippers, scattering the pigeons that roost in the tower. The bell rope is thick and knotted and mysteriously recoils through a hole in the ceiling after each tug. I grasp the rope with both hands and lever it back and forth, back and forth. The sound is deafening, the loudest noise I know other that the siren from the fire department that blares a beckoning call to the volunteers whenever there's a blaze out of control.

I find the kitchen matches in the sacristy and light my torch. I approach the altar, remembering to bow, and light the three candles on either side of the cross. Joe has arrived by now, and I notice again the stubble on his chin, which contrasts sharply with my peach-fuzzed face. He gathers the cross as he is older and is to lead the procession. We head out the side door to congregate with the choir and Dr. Tayloe at the front of the church.

Goronwy and Me

We greet the familiar worshippers, including my family, and my mother pauses to pat down my unruly hair before proceeding into the church.

At eleven o'clock, Dr. Tayloe nods, and Joe leads us into the narthex. Edith Buford, the organist, sees him from her perch behind the choir stall, adjusts her glasses, and begins her weekly battle with our wheezy organ. The opening strains of "A Mighty Fortress is Our God" are announced, and Joe lifts high the cross to begin the procession. Carrying the torch, I am behind his right shoulder, and I am startled when behind me, the choir starts singing. We march in and I wince, as the elderly ladies of the choir struggle with their failing eyesight and cacophonous voices to synch their singing with Mrs. Buford's playing. We reach the altar, and the choir files into their seats. Joe and I bow to the cross and retire to our station, ready for another of Dr. Tayloe's ponderous sermons on a vengeful Old Testament God.

The service is unremarkable, familiar as I am with the weekly vicissitudes of our worship. Right on cue, Granny arrives after the procession and during the reading of the first lesson, and without haste, walks to our accustomed pew, third from the front on the gospel side of the aisle. I have long stopped being embarrassed by her habitual yet premeditated tardiness, and I admit to myself that my grandmother does indeed look stunning in her tailored suit and Sara Sue hat acquired, no doubt, during one of her many forays to Richmond to shop at Miller & Rhoads and Montaldos.

I resolve to listen to Dr. Tayloe's sermon, but am soon lost in his discursive lesson on the history of the Philistines and pray instead for good reception on our GE television for the afternoon's game between Sonny Jurgensen's Redskins and the Eagles of Norm Snead, and, as a Redskins fan, I again offer thanks to God for this providential trade of franchise quarterbacks. Near the sermon's end, I nudge Joe as he indeed has fallen asleep and his labored breathing has the potential to erupt into full-throated snores. During the offertory hymn, June Thomas, the most near-sighted and tone-deaf member of the choir, inexplicably, but predictably, skips verse two to passionately belt out verse three, while the rest of the choristers and the congregation soldier on as the hymnist intended. Remarkably, everyone comes together by the song's end. I imagine God is not terribly inconvenienced by this transgression.

As the small band of parishioners kneel at the altar during communion, I note with interest the deep draughts of wine gulped by Raymond Bradley, such a sharp contrast to the chaste sips of the other penitents. Perhaps he needs to be cleansed of manifold sins, I think.

I Meet Goronwy Owen

Dr. Tayloe offers a final prayer, and as Mrs. Buford launches into "Onward Christian Soldiers," Joe and I lead the recessional down the center aisle and out the front door so we may all "do the work God intended us to do." As Dr. Tayloe greets the departing parishioners, Joe and I circle around the side door to finish our duties. He secures the cross and before I even finish extinguishing the candles, he hangs up his robe and surplice and leaves, eager, I imagine, to keep a date with Miss October.

I wander out to the church yard, knowing it will be minutes yet before we go to Granny's, the men having to arrange their afternoon foursomes, while my mother chats with ladies from the county that she sees only at meetings of the altar guild and the garden club. The sun is indeed warm now at its daily zenith, and I seek the shade of the reverential oaks and their burnt-orange leaves. I'm drawn to the white Celtic cross on the edge of the church lot, and I place my palm against its cool white granite.

Of course, I am familiar with the monument, having rested at its base many times over the years, and I know the name of the man it honors. I know he was a poet and clergyman from Wales who somehow ended up in Brunswick County. And from reading the inscription, I know he was (is) held in high esteem by certain people or groups of people. But now, as my family emerges from the cluster of departing worshippers, I wonder, perhaps for the first time, exactly who is Goronwy Owen?

2

I Meet Goronwy Again

**REST IN PEACE
by Proal Heartwell**

    Two or three times a year, now,
    I polish my shoes, unearth my dark suit,
    And with my wife, drive the back roads of Virginia
    To the town where I was born.

    There, on a hill above the railroad tracks,
    I gather with erstwhile friends
    And bear silent witness to a life that was
    As we bury another member of our parents' generation.

    In the distance is the field where we used to play ball
    On teams of our own choosing and with our own rules
    And means of settling disputes.

    We are a team again, as we carry the coffin,
    Moving in unison, knowing our fathers would shoulder the task,
    If only they could.

I Meet Goronwy Again

After, we congregate at some ancestral home
On the way to ruin with its irredeemable furnace, plaster walls,
And ghostly memories.

We eat angel food cake, drink a beer, recall simpler times,
And lie, saying we would come back if only we could,
Fix up the old place and live like kings.

Our wives, who we met in college and who come from cities,
Glance at one another in alarm
And laugh nervously.

We say good-bye, promise to visit before the next sad occasion.
I drive through town, slowly,
Vigilant for some reversal of perceptible decay.
Each street, each block, is ripe with memories
And I spill them upon my wife.
That is where I wrecked my bike,
That is where I first kissed Pam,
There, where we all played kick-the-can
Well past dark, knowing our parents knew
We were safe.

My wife nods and pats my arm, but she doesn't know,
She couldn't, and I chide myself for my sentimentality.

We take the quick way home, on the interstate,
Where each mile looks the same,
And the cars in front of us drive on the sun
Resting on the mountains.

Goronwy and Me

TIME PASSES. I DO go to Woodberry Forest where I score no touchdowns against St. Christopher's, or anyone else. I go to college, and in my first year, my parents move from our little hometown, the town, indeed the street, where my father had lived his entire life, excepting his own years in college and his service in the Navy during World War II.

More time passes. I graduate, try a number of different jobs before beginning my career as a teacher at age thirty. Susie and I marry; two years later our daughter Elise is born, and life assumes a generally comfortable rhythm. Trips to Lawrenceville are infrequent now: once for Granny's funeral and once to show off the baby Elise to my parents' friends who, after all, have known me since the day I was born.

I grow older and, perhaps not surprisingly, nostalgic for my former hometown, where increasingly I realize, I experienced a largely idyllic childhood. When Elise enters high school, I determine it is time to take her on a self-proclaimed "roots tour," and on a sunny Saturday in October we set off for Brunswick County to visit the haunts of my youth, and, as an added enticement, stop by the annual Brunswick Stew Festival. A brief aside about Brunswick Stew: Brunswick Stew is an inextricable part of my childhood memories. In my mind, I still see the men of the Ruritan Club stirring with boat paddles big kettles of the concoction over an open fire on cool fall mornings at a vacant lot near the fire department. After simmering for hours, the stew is ladled into cardboard quart containers, and my mother buys several to freeze and then thaw and heat on cold Sunday nights in the winter before the family settles in to watch "The Ed Sullivan Show." I loved (and love) the rich mixture of sweetly collapsed tomatoes, corn, and lima beans happily commingling with tender chicken and spicy black pepper. Add some saltine crackers, and, in my estimation, you have no room for complaint. Today, sadly, my encounters with Brunswick Stew usually involve a big yellow can. Now, Mrs. Fearnow does a fair job with her product, but it definitely lacks the smoky richness of the Ruritans' stew.

Now despite the claims of the fine folks of Brunswick, Georgia, there can be no doubt that Brunswick Stew traces its roots to my home in Brunswick County, Virginia. Consider this excerpt from the *Brunswick Story: A History of Brunswick County* (published in 1957) by Edith Rathburn Bell and William Lightfoot Heartwell, Jr., my father:

> To Brunswick County belongs the honor of originating an epicurean delight of national renown. This could only be Brunswick Stew, which is served (mostly erroneously) on menus across the

I Meet Goronwy Again

breadth of the land. Brunswick Stew is a byword among the natives of the county, and although it is not prepared as often as in the past, it still serves as the main dish at practically every civic or social outdoor gathering in the county.

There has always been some contention as to the exact place where this famous dish was first made. Some contend that it was on the banks of the Meherrin, but early accounts seem to verify the fact that it was first cooked in Red Oak district on the banks of the Nottoway.

It has been called "Haskin's stew," "Matthew's stew," and quite simply, "squirrel stew." The general consensus is that it was first made by an old man, "Uncle Jimmy" Matthews, who was a retainer of Dr. Creed Haskins who lived at Mount Donum on the Nottoway River. The original recipe included no vegetables and the basic ingredients of all of the early recipes were practically the same, although some added old brandy or Madeira wine to give the stew a flavor.

In all recipes squirrel was the main ingredient. The original stew was described in a letter by Mr. Meade Haskins as follows: "Parboil squirrels until they are stiff (half done), cut small slices of bacon (middling). One for each squirrel; one small onion to each squirrel chopped up. Put in bacon and onions first to boil, while the squirrels are being cut up for the pot. Boil the above till half done, then put in butter to taste; then stale loaf bread, crumbled up. Cook then till it bubbles, then add pepper and salt to taste. Cook this until it bubbles and bubbles burst off. Time for stew to cook is four hours with steady heat."

Today, chicken and lamb have replaced squirrel and many cooks add vegetables and have replaced the stale bread with cracker crumbs. The consistency of the stew, good and thick, might remain the same, but old timers will swear "it just ain't the same." Regardless, it is a dish that still makes for mighty good eating and remains a solid favorite in its home county of Brunswick.[1]

There you have it. Case closed.

So back to the roots tour. Elise convinces her friends Emilia and Suzannah to accompany us on this excursion, reasonably concluding, I suspect, that her father's stories would be more palatable with friends along to share her chagrin. I love these girls, but at the time, the three of them are deep in rehearsals for the fall production of their high school's musical, *Les Miserables*. As we set off from Charlottesville, the girls launch into the

---

1. Bell and Heartwell, *Brunswick Story*, 77.

overture and they proceed to sing the complete score as we drive through the pine trees and red clay of Southside Virginia. Now I admire Jean Valjean as much as the next man, and the story of little Cosette will truly break your heart, but I admit to being much relieved as we approached the outskirts of Lawrenceville. During the drive, in the moments between songs when the girls are catching their breath, I tell them (and remind Susie) that Lawrenceville is a sleepy town, and as such not to expect too much. In fact, I inform them, there is only one stoplight in town, indeed in all of Brunswick County, on the corner of Main and Church Streets.

And as we enter town on Windsor Avenue, all seems quiet. We pull over in front of my old house, the house where my parents raised four children and lived for over thirty years. Built in 1895 and formerly a boarding house for railroad workers, it doesn't look bad, and I point out my bedroom window above the front porch that loops around the building's southeast side. The back yard is smaller now, the current owners having ceded to scrub cedars and kudzu a large swath of space that formerly served as a field for games of touch football and where my father, my brother, and I vainly tried to tame erratic golf swings.

Across the street sits the tattered home of the deceased Edith Buford, church organist and grandmother of our good Charlottesville friend, Bliss Abbot. Bliss grew up in Richmond, but fondly remembers visits she and sister Peyton took to "E's" home. Morning play was followed by a nap, and, in the afternoon, the girls would put on their best dresses and, after "E" applied rouge to their respective cheeks, the girls would accompany their grandmother to Allen's Drug Store for fountain Cokes over crushed ice.

We slowly drive on down the street, past Granny's house. The two-story columns on the front porch are decayed and peeling, and Granny's beloved magnolia and crape myrtle trees are gone. We round the curve, Joe Bradley's house on the left, towards Church Street only to encounter something I had never experienced in Lawrenceville: a traffic jam. We later learn that it is St. Paul's homecoming, and we, apparently, have now stumbled onto the end of the homecoming parade. These parades were a cherished spectacle of fall afternoons in my childhood. Main Street and Church Street were closed as rudimentary floats transporting the homecoming court rolled by. I don't recall if St. Paul's had a marching band; I think the homecoming game opponent usually provided this staple parade element. I remember one year watching the parade from the second floor window of Raymond Bradley's store as Joe aimed his pea shooter at the

I Meet Goronwy Again

drum major from Virginia Union, Fayetteville State, or some other school of the Central Intercollegiate Athletic Conference.

Today, cars are not moving as up ahead we witness a vehicular standoff at the gates of the college. Parade traffic, game traffic, and unsuspecting county farmers and wives on routine Saturday shopping excursions have made the lower end of Windsor Avenue impassable.

Having lost all credibility with the girls ("I thought you said Lawrenceville was a sleepy town …"), we extricate ourselves from the traffic by turning right onto Purdy Street, at the base of which sits the two-story brick structure where I attended elementary school and which also housed the high school in my father's day. I remember the desks bolted into the well-oiled wooden floors, the framed portraits of George Washington in every classroom, and the alphabet—upper case and lower case letters—written in cursive on lined green cardboard stretching above the blackboard. I still hear the whole school—all seven grades—singing "Up on the Rooftop" at Christmas while standing on the massive central staircase in the front hallway, and the shouts of my friends engaged in another epic kickball game on the asphalt playground. I tell the girls how as a child I walked home everyday for lunch where Ruth, our maid, ceased her ironing to prepare for me tomato soup and a grilled cheese sandwich. I then returned to school and the cafeteria to exchange a nickel for a Brown Mule ice cream bar to be enjoyed under the towering oaks of the schoolyard. I would rejoin my classmates in the room of one of our spinster teachers who instructed us in Virginia history, and, who, also, somehow managed to engender in some of us an abiding love of poetry.

We drive the two blocks to Oak Hill Cemetery, where we get out of the van to stretch our legs. We walk over the crest of the hill to the shaded Heartwell family plot where rest my grandparents, my Aunt Margaret, and, most recently, my father. Across the street sits Pigeon Hill, where my father and his friends played baseball as boys. The railroad track skirts the bottom of the hill, and as the story goes, Daddy once hit a ball into an open boxcar en route to San Francisco, declaring it was the longest home run ever hit. Well, maybe. We pick a few weeds and decide to drive out into the county to give the town traffic time to dissipate.

We head first to the site of Fort Christanna, built in 1714 by colonial governor Alexander Spotswood and designed to promote settlement in the regions inhabited by the Sappony, Nottoway, and Meherrin tribes. The fort also housed a schoolhouse for Indian children where, apparently, they learned to read the Bible and Common Prayers, and to write and speak English. When I was a child, my family sometimes picnicked at this site on the banks of the Meherrin River, and I remember the amazement I experienced when my mother, the quintessential southern belle from Mobile, Alabama, borrowed my Uncle Jack's .22 and deftly shot a succession of tin cans off a table-top boulder in the middle of a sloping plain. She learned her skills in marksmanship as a teenager when she spent a summer in the mountains of North Carolina recovering from scarlet fever and where, incredibly, I was told she also learned to square dance. Go figure.

Then, and now, all that remains of this former fort is a cannon barrel ensconced in a concrete pedestal. We read the inscription, note the beer cans stuffed in the cannon's mouth, and take a few pictures. We head back towards town, detouring slightly as I search for the block building that once housed the *Lawrenceville Advertiser*, a weekly newspaper where I worked the summer I was sixteen. I find the building, now the office of a lumber company, and in the parking lot I tell the girls that it was here that I lost the first joint of my middle finger when I caught my hand in a printing press. For Elise, Suzannah, and Emilia, this is clearly the highlight of the trip, as the story provides requisite amounts of blood and gore. In fact, Elise is so impressed that she gets out of the van to snap a picture of the offending building.

All is quiet now in town when we park in front of the courthouse just a few yards from the intersection of Main Street and Hicks Street. At the head of this intersection is a furniture store in what was once Thomas Hardware, my grandfather's business, where as a child I would ride my bike to whenever I needed a baseball or Mother required a light bulb. Inside the store were kegs of nails, walls of nuts and bolts with a ladder on tracks to retrieve items from the top shelves, and men in bib overalls swapping stories.

We walk down Main Street, and I point out the old library, site of ritualistic Saturday forays in search of any book that might garner my affection as much as *Kon Tiki* which I devoured cover to cover when I was in seventh grade. We get back in the van to drive the few blocks to St. Andrew's Episcopal Church. This is our last stop before heading to the grounds of the Brunswick Stew Festival, where we will sample and buy offerings from several stew masters and where the girls will dine on such culinary delights as deep-fried Snickers and Twinkies.

We pull into the small gravel lot at St. Andrew's and once again disembark. The church is locked, but the girls listen respectfully (I had been, after

I Meet Goronwy Again

all, their English teacher for four years in middle school) as I go through the litany of duties from my days as an acolyte.

We are hungry now, and the stew beckons. We walk back towards the van when a white Celtic cross catches Elise's eye. She goes over to take a closer look, and as I wait by the driver's side door, she calls out, "Hey, Dad, who is Goronwy Owen?"

3

Who is Goronwy Owen?

FROM CYWYDD MOLAWD MÔN (CYWYDD OF PRAISE FOR ANGLESEY)
by Goronwy Owen

Hail Anglesey, lovely land, the most beauteous of all regions: a rich land, the second Eden, the pristine Paradise. You have been elegantly endowed. Loved one of God and man: a comely island protected by the sea's battlements. You occupy a dazzling throne, second to none. Your every corner is luxurious, lady and mistress of the sea. The season's miracles transform you in their time, queenly isle. No other land, mighty isle, is comparable for splendour, abundance and opulence— rich in mines, dales, meads and beaches, bread and cheese, beer and meat, fish, fowl, and herds. Your fertile leafy meadows are heavy with crops like an ancient Carmel. Oh, how thick, my dear Anglesey, are the fleeces of your flocks, which, when shorn, clothe you elegantly ... Your priests and laymen are learned saints of sincere beliefs and steadfast faith. In place of malice, oppression, and arrogance you will abound with all good virtues. True trust and loving kindness, a plenitude of unity and righteousness to love and glorify God. The Lord above will christen you His Little Garden and all the peoples of the earth will recognize your greatness. In greatness, virtue and renown you will remain an eternal wonder.

Who is Goronwy Owen?

WHEN YOU "GOOGLE" THE name Goronwy Owen, the first site that pops up is Wikipedia, the free encyclopedia, which declares that, "Goronwy Owen (1 January 1723–July 1769) was one of the eighteenth century's greatest Welsh poets." The entry goes on to note that

> he mastered the traditional bardic metres and, although forced by circumstance to be an exile, played an important role in the literary and antiquarian movement in Wales often described as the Welsh Eighteenth Century Renaissance. A perfectionist who only published reluctantly and whose literary output is consequently relatively small, his work nevertheless had a huge influence on Welsh poetry for several generations and his poetic genius and tragic life gave him a cult status in Welsh literary circles.

Reading this entry, I am immediately struck by several phrases. Anecdotally, I certainly already knew that Owen was a great Welsh poet, but I knew nothing of "traditional bardic metres." I teach my students about iambic pentameter, but I'm guessing "bardic metres" is somehow far removed from the clean rhythm of the Shakespearean sonnet.

I wonder also about the phrase "forced by circumstance to be an exile." What are these circumstances, and am I to believe that Brunswick County is the place of his exile? To me, "exile" suggests he had no choice in the matter. Wasn't Napoleon exiled to Elba after his abdication? Wasn't Prospero cast out to sea and exiled on a deserted island by his usurpers, including his evil brother Antonio? I'm curious to learn how events transpired to lead this "great" poet to what was once my home.

Additionally, I'm intrigued by the notation that Owen was "perfectionist who published only reluctantly." This seems paradoxical to me as most writers I know crave the recognition that comes with publication. After all, how can your work be appreciated when the public has no access to it?

Finally, I am sobered by the concluding mention that "his poetic genius and tragic life gave him a cult status in Welsh literary circles." It seems clear that I must endeavor to understand Owen's poetic genius while simultaneously exploring his tragic life. But what of the cult status? Will I, too, drink the Kool-Aid if, and when, I become a disciple?

The official website for Brunswick County also contains information on Owen who "spent his last years in Brunswick County, as rector from 1761 to 1769 of the colonial St. Andrews parish." Tourbrunswick.org goes on to mention that Owen wrote his last poem in the county, "an elegy for a Welsh friend . . . remarkable for its use of ancient Welsh poetic devices." More bardic metres, I suppose.

The site describes Owen's life as "tempestuous" which, perhaps, is a notch above "tragic" and says that, "twice-widowed, Owen married a third wife in Brunswick County, and acquired a small cotton and tobacco plantation. A colonial style dwelling is still on the property." What is known of this third wife, I wonder. What happened to the first two? And I'm amazed to learn that his Brunswick County home may still be standing 241 years after his death.

The website goes on to say that, "only in the twentieth century did scholars and clergymen rediscover the story of Goronwy Owen in Virginia. Rev. Edwin T. Williams and Mrs. Loyd V. Bell, Jr. were active in this research in Brunswick County."

Wow, now this is interesting. I know that Rev. Williams baptized me, although he was gone from St. Andrew's by the time I started acolyting. And, of course, I remember Mrs. Bell. She was active in the church, and her children were friends of ours growing up. She taught seventh grade at Lawrenceville Elementary School, and her husband coached me in JV football my one and only year at Brunswick High School. Mrs. Bell also co-authored the *Brunswick Story* with my father. (My father was always the first to admit that Edie Bell did most of the research and writing.) Was Mrs. Bell still alive, I wondered, and what did she really know of Goronwy Owen?

Brunswick Story: A History of Brunswick County is a curious publication, "written at the request of the board of supervisors, Brunswick County, Virginia, in observance of the 350th anniversary of the settlement of Jamestown." It is my understanding that all counties of the Commonwealth were commissioned to write similar histories to present to young Elizabeth II during her official visit to England's former colony. My father was the chairman of the Jamestown Committee for Brunswick County, and in the forward of the book he proclaimed that, "in the preparation of this work the committee has sincerely tried to present a short and colorful narrative of events from the entry of the first white man until the present day." He goes on to acknowledge the efforts of Mrs. Bell, who "has worked tirelessly, and with inspiration, and has catalogued information on our county that would produce a thick volume. This information," Daddy writes, "will be filed in the clerk's office with the hope that some future historian will compile a more comprehensive history of Brunswick County and have it published."[1]

---

1. Bell and Heartwell, *Brunswick Story*, 7.

Who is Goronwy Owen?

In the course of sixty-five pages, *Brunswick Story* delineates the history "of one of the Commonwealth's oldest and most illustrious counties." It highlights notable events and concisely portrays various aspects of county living during the preceding three hundred years. The tone, it seems to me, reflects the time during which the book was written. For example, there is little discussion of slavery and certainly no acknowledgement of the evils of the "peculiar institution." *Brunswick Story* is an engaging, informative read, and a work that I'm sure received approbation from the board of supervisors (and the Chamber of Commerce). The Queen's assessment is not known.

A small portion of the text deals with the history of St. Andrew's Parish and of Goronwy Owen. In six short paragraphs, it is explained that in 1760 the vestry asked Gov. Fauquier for permission to "test" two potential rectors, Patrick Lunan and Goronwy Owen. Apparently the vestry was unimpressed with both candidates, and decided to retain neither after the probationary period. However, the Governor intervened on Owen's behalf and "his pay was in pounds of tobacco which was the currency of the period." When Owen died nine years later, Brunswick Story notes that "he had an extensive library, which included books in Greek and Latin, Hebrew, Welsh and French, as well as English. These were items not usually found in the homes of the period," the section concludes.[2] Wow, talk about an understatement!

My father's desire "that some future historian will compile a more comprehensive history of Brunswick" was fulfilled nearly twenty years after the publication of *Brunswick Story*. *Brunswick County, Virginia: 1720–1975* by Gay Neale was created under the auspices of the Brunswick County Bicentennial Committee. (We sure like anniversaries in this country!) The book is certainly "more comprehensive" than the one penned by Daddy and Mrs. Bell, and, in my opinion, it is distinguished by its nearly two hundred pages of appendices which include "First Land Grants and Patents in Brunswick County"; "Marriage Bonds and Minister's Returns, 1790 to 1810"; as well as listings of the members of the colonial militia, census records from 1810, and records of soldiers from the county in the Civil War, World War I, and World War II. These and other appendices represent a treasure trove of minutiae for those, like me, who are interested in tracing family history.

---

2. Ibid., 30.

Goronwy and Me

In her book, Ms. Neale presents more information on the life and career of Goronwy Owen. She recaps the events leading to the minister's "call" to Brunswick County and reveals that his annual salary was sixteen thousand pounds of tobacco. She traces Owen's "paradoxical" life and notes that he was ordained to the ministry in Wales in 1746. She asserts that he was a classical scholar, "quoting from the Greek and Latin classics with ease," and she acknowledges that Owen's "poetry does not translate well in English; the style that Owen perfected relies on intricate alliteration and masterful use of the Welsh Language."[3]

According to Ms. Neale, there is only one surviving poem penned by Owen during his years in Brunswick County, an ode in memory of his friend and patron Lewis Morris, which presents a less than flattering depiction of Brunswick County:

> The land of woods and of wild hills, the forested land
> Of every kind of heinous insect;
> The Ugly land of murderous people—
> Indians, strange lot, I am sorry to say. [4]

Ms. Neale points out that there was apparently little affection between Owen and his parishioners. He wrote in a letter, "may God and his saints protect me from its [Brunswick's] inhabitants, apart from those that are English; and not all of those are good." According to the author, Owen's "parish treated him in a cool manner. He was soon forgotten after his death, and his grave remained unmarked for almost two centuries."[5]

Ms. Neale concludes, "Owen's is a tragic story. In a day of aggressive men and hard drinking, his weakness and scholarly nature, coupled with his addiction to alcohol, led to disaster. He could not succeed in the position open to him; the life of a poet was not a practical one. But out of this life that ended sadly after forty-six years came a gift to the world: the poetry that is cherished by the Welsh people today. And this man known throughout his life, especially during his nine years in Brunswick, as an unsuccessful, alcoholic minister, is world-renowned as a poetic genius."[6]

What is it about alcohol and poetry, I wonder. Certainly literary history is strewn with accounts of writers fueled (and consumed) by alcohol. As

---

3. Neale, *Brunswick County*, 90.
4. Ibid., 91.
5. Ibid., 89.
6. Ibid., 92–93.

an example, we need look no further than Virginia's Edgar Allan Poe who was a member of the Brunswick Society while at the University of Virginia, and who visited the eponymous county during his college days. And there's Dylan Thomas, Owen's fellow countryman whose struggles with alcohol are legendary. Perhaps there is something about the creative process and its often debilitating search for truth that requires numbing from the real world. Or, perhaps, as Ms. Neale suggests, it is "weakness."

The connection between Owen's art and his dissolute living is further explored in John Gwilym Jones's *Goronwy Owen's Virginian Adventure: His Life, Poetry, and Literary Opinion, With a Translation of His Virginian Letters*. Published in 1969, this booklet begins,

> Candor compels a critic to acknowledge Goronwy Owen's pathetic, almost tragic weakness of character. In that stocky dark-bearded Welshman charm and geniality rubbed shoulder with the most abject scrounging, an obsessive affection for his wife and children with an equally obsessive urge for degrading drinking orgies, a genuine love for his native Welsh language with an almost complete disuse of it on his native hearth. But moral aberrations as such are no barriers to poetic achievement.[7]

Indeed.

I first encountered this publication while perusing the bookshelves of my mother's home a few years ago at the beginning of my self-proclaimed obsession with Owen. Mother doesn't recall where the booklet came from; it's one of five hundred copies hand printed and bound, and it was published by the Botetourt Bibliographical Society, whose "general purpose . . . is to make available a series of annual checklists of eighteenth-century Virginia libraries."

As his opening sentence suggests, Jones is no apologist for Owen's behavior, and to some extent, he "de-mythologizes" the poet's work by placing it in the context of his better-known contemporaries. Jones gives a brief overview of Owen's life before exploring the literary tradition that influenced him. He then goes on to explain "the unique structures of traditional Welsh poetry" favored and perfected by Owen. For example, he looks at Owen's use of cynghannedd, "a system of Welsh prosody [that] has no English equivalent, in fact, no equivalent in any language." Jones further illuminates Owen's use of meter (aha, the traditional bardic metre) by focusing on the cywydd , "the measure almost invariably practiced by

---

7. Jones, *Virginian Adventure*, 3.

Goronwy and Me

Goronwy." According to Jones, "the cywydd consists of a series of rhymed couplets with seven syllables in each line—about thirty seems to be the prevalent length, though length can vary considerably. Every line must contain a cynghannedd, and one of the rhymes must be a monosyllable and the other a polysyllable." Jones further states, "the cywydd, in time, was almost exclusively eulogistic, singing the praises of the gentry, the beloved, or the lord, in hyperbole with idealized comparison."[8]

Jones finds certain of Owen's poems "patently imitative," but concludes, "whatever Goronwy's shortcomings are, he never falters architecturally. All of his poems have a beginning, a middle, and an end. The development is simple, maybe, but his sense of form is invariably exquisitely precise and logical."[9]

Jones also makes mention of Owen's last poem, an ode containing all twenty-four measures, written in memory of his friend and patron, Lewis Morris. "This ode was written after 1765 in Virginia and contains a reference to that fact: 'Though it is a wearisome journey from this country thither [i.e. England] over the foamy deep, the awkwardness of sad greetings no land can hinder, no wave kill.'"[10]

After looking at several other of Owen's poems, Jones concludes his study with this assessment of Owen: "a basically tough and genial personality of undoubted spasmodic genius who found himself in a world beyond his gifts to control."[11]

Gorowny Owen's Virginian Letters are appended to Jones's study. These three epistles reveal in vivid prose the dire circumstances confronting Owen as he prepares to leave England; his first experiences on board the aptly named *Trial*; and years later, an accounting of his life in Brunswick.

The first letter, dated November 2, 1757, is addressed "To the honourable and venerable Society of Cymmrodorion, Goronwy Ddu [Goronwy the Black], their friend and once Bard and Servant till Death sends his greeting." The Honourable Society of Cymmrodorion is a literary society devoted to the preservation of the Welsh language and culture. Founded in London in 1751 by brothers Lewis and Richard Morris, the society's secretary was once Goronwy Owen, who also hoped the group would pay him "for ministering in Welsh" in "some church or chapel once a Sunday."

8. Ibid., 10–11.
9. Ibid., 19.
10. Ibid., 22.
11. Ibid., 26.

Who is Goronwy Owen?

This hope was not realized, although the society was very kind to him. In the letter Owen explains that he is reluctantly embarking to Virginia for the sake of his family. Owen had been offered a teaching position in the Grammar School at the College of William and Mary. There, he will be paid two hundred pounds a year, which "far exceeds anything that I ever expected in Britain or Ireland; and how could I justify myself to my family if I refused the offer through cowardice or indifference?" At the present, however, Owen acknowledges that "after coming to terms with the owner of the ship, I realize that all the money available for the journey, and all that I possess (having cleared all my debt) are scarcely enough to meet the cost of my passage . . ." Therefore, Owen continues, "I appeal to you . . . to assist me now in such dire need. I doubt not the good will of any of you in the crisis; but whether of not you consent to consider my condition, I pray God to bestow success upon you in this world, and the world to come—this at present being all your obedient servant is capable of."[12]

One month later (December 12, 1757), Owen writes to Richard Morris ("Dear Compatriot") while on board the *Trial* at Spithead. He begins, "We have arrived thus far, through the Providence of the Most High, in good health without mishap or pain or sea-sickness or any other misfortune to hinder us, though the weather was often cold and stormy while we were in the Downs and from the Downs here. My wife and three little Welshmen have been wonderfully courageous and without either sea-sickness or nausea, apart from a slight light-headedness the day we left the Nore for the Downs . . ." Ironically, Owen's good fortune would not last: on the voyage to Virginia, his wife and the youngest of his "three little Welshmen" both died.

Owen goes on in this letter to berate the sailors, "horrible, filthy men. As God is my witness, every one of them has taken for himself a mistress from among the she-thieves and do no work but copulate wantonly in every corner of the ship." He reserves particular disgust for the captain ("there never lived a worse brute") and condemns him (and his "concubine") for imbibing wine and ale while his passengers must "drink fetid water or choke." Owen fears that the captain will so anger him, "that I shall run my sword under his ribs and thank him for giving me such a big sharp-pointed weapon."[13]

The final letter, again to Richard Morris, is written nearly ten years later in Brunswick County. Dated July 23, 1767, this missive details how

12. Ibid., 27–29.
13. Ibid., 29–30.

Goronwy and Me

Owen came to learn of Lewis Morris' death. He also characterizes, "most of the population of this place [as] descendants of thieves from every country, and have a devilish itch in their fingers to interfere with other people's property and to know all the goings that passes between a native Englishman and his compatriots in England. They have an insatiable urge to know the affairs of the men from Britain, and whether or not they give good reports of their county and its people in their letters to their fellow country-men." However, Owen further relates that, "I am (God be praised) healthy and active, and this country suits me well enough. Not one of my English family is alive except my son Robert, and he is an adult as I am. I am married to my third wife and have three children born here besides Robin."

Owen concludes this letter inquiring after mutual acquaintances (including his sister) in Wales and finishes with, "May God remain with you. I shall expect a letter in six months time. I am yours etc., Goronwy Owen."[14] Owen died almost exactly two years after the date of this letter.

I find these letters extraordinary. I am moved by the immediacy of their prose, their vibrancy of language, and urgency of feeling. There is a palpable, desperate sense of longing and sublimation, and I do applaud Owen for his courage to travel to this unknown land. True, his courage was born of financial hardship, but he nonetheless resolved to act and he followed through on this resolve. How many of us would dare to do the same?

By now, I am gaining a fuller picture of Owen and his life (tragic? tempestuous?). I have a better sense of his longing for Wales, and the circumstances that required him to be absent from it. To learn more of the poet's complex life, I return to the Internet. Now, I am not particularly savvy when it comes to navigating the World Wide Web. In fact, a student once referred to me as "the man technology left behind." But as I begin to explore the world of cyberspace, I discover some incredible resources. Take, for example, an article published on Owen in January, 1901 in the *William and Mary Quarterly*. Written by Dr. Lyon G. Tyler, the president of the college, the article begins, "Poetry rarely blossoms in new countries, where the struggle for subsistence or wealth absorbs the public attention. Nevertheless, it may be interesting to know that Virginia has been the residence of the three greatest poets who have lived on this continent for any length of time. Each century since foundation of the state has had its genius in poetry."[15] (Take that, you New England "Fireside Poets"!)

14. Ibid., 30–31.
15. Tyler, "Goronwy Owen," 152.

Who is Goronwy Owen?

Dr. Tyler explains:

> In his room in Capt. Pierce's home at Jamestown, surrounded by his silkworms, George Sandys (uncle of Sir Francis Wyatt), whom Dryden pronounced "the best verifier of his age," turned the Latin of Ovid into exquisite verse.
>
> The eighteenth century welcomed to Virginia the master spirit of Goronwy Owen, whose ode to his dear friend, Lewis Morris, written in the backwoods of Virginia, is pronounced by competent critics of Welsh verse a marvelous piece of mechanism and heart-stirring poetry.
>
> In the nineteenth century lived Edgar Allen [sic] Poe, who spent his youth and received his education in Virginia, and who, in all the essential elements of a poet's character, easily holds the first place among American-born poets.[16]

Dr. Tyler then points out, "But the particular subject of this article is Goronwy Owen, whose name, though resplendent among his countrymen, is hardly known among even educated Americans." Then, in the course of fifteen pages, Dr. Tyler seeks to instruct us. He gives us details about Owen's parents, characterizing his father as a "reckless ne'er do well" but noting that his mother "taught him the pure use of his native tongue, and sowed in the genial soil of his young mind the seeds of which in after years produced such rich harvest."[17] The author goes on to tell of Owen's friendship with the Morris brothers and his formal education.

Dr. Tyler touches upon Owen's life at William and Mary by asserting that "little is known, save that he married Mrs. Clayton, sister of President Thomas Dawson, and she was his second wife. He remained two years, when he resigned..."[18]

This resignation, Dr. Tyler writes, "is said to have been due to the merry habits of Mr. Owen, which induced him and Mr. Jacob Rowe, professor of moral philosophy, to lead the students in a row with the young men of the town."[19] The Board of Visitors and Governors dismissed Mr. Rowe and Owen resigned to avoid a similar fate.

It was then that Owen was called to St. Andrew's Parish in Brunswick County. According to Dr. Tyler,

---

16. Ibid., 152.
17. Ibid., 152–53.
18. Ibid., 153.
19. Ibid., 154.

> The people of Brunswick County were not scholars like Goronwy, but they were not as illiterate as the generality of the people of England at this time. There was no pauper class in Brunswick. John Lightfoot drove with his coach and six horses, and major Nathaniel Edwards had his "double chair" and the people generally were comfortably fixed. Drinking and swearing were doubtless vices here as elsewhere in Virginia, but they were not carried to the excess that Goronwy Owen and his friends had carried them in England. The evidence is conclusive that Owen fared much better in Brunswick than he ever did in any of the parishes of Wales or England. He had a good salary, a comfortable home, his horses, and his negroes.[20]

Dr. Tyler, too, speaks of the requiem to Lewis Morris that Owen wrote in Brunswick County which "is not only touching in the depth of its pathos, but it accomplishes one of the greatest literary feats connected with the Welsh language. It is written in each of the four and twenty bardic metres [Agggh!], and, what makes the performance almost marvelous technically, every line terminates with the same syllable."[21]

Next, Dr. Tyler summarizes Owen's three marriages and goes on to give a detailed account of his descendents based on a piece by Dr. Whyte Glendower Owen written for *The Columbia* and published March 10, 1892. I am astonished to learn that one of Goronwy Owen's sons and several of his grandchildren ended up in Mobile, Alabama. Mobile is the hometown to my mother, Lucy Dorgan, whose family shares a long history with the port city. Owen's descendants distinguished themselves in Mobile: one was a Congressman, one was mayor of the city, one was "collector of the port." Several were educated at the University of Alabama (as were my grandparents) and fought for the Confederacy in the War Between the States. In fact, a little digging reveals that George W. Owen, great-grandson of the poet served in the Mobile Cadets with Capt. Augustus Proal Dorgan, my great-great-grandfather. Both saw action at Shiloh, where Private Owen was wounded. Wow!

In his article, Dr. Tyler also includes extracts from the Vestry Book of St. Andrew's Parish, which gives insight into Owen's tenure ministering in the "backwoods" of Brunswick, and "the Records show that he attended nearly every one of the Vestry meetings during his incumbency."[22]

20. Ibid.," 154–55.
21. Ibid., 155.
22. Ibid.

From the Order Books of Brunswick County, Dr. Tyler presents the following:

> Brunswick County the twenty-seventh Day of May 1765. The Grand Jury returned the following presentment to-writ: The Reverend Gorowny Owen for getting drunk. The same for profane swearing, By the information of John Maclin Sen.

At a Court &c. 27 day of July 1765

> The Reverend Gorowny Owen who stands presented by the Grand Jury for getting drunk having been duly served with a copy of said presentment, is considered that for the said offence he forfeit and pay to the church warden of St. Andrews parish where said offence was committed five shillings or fifty pounds of tobacco to the use of the poor of said parish and that he pay the court for this prosecution, and may be taken &c.[23]

Ouch!

Dr. Tyler concludes his article with Owen's will, dated July 3, 1769. He gives to his "dearly beloved wife Iona Owen the plantation and land where my dwelling house is, during her life and after her decease to be equally divided among my four sons namely, Robert Owen, Richard Brown Owen, Gorowny Owen, and John Lloyd Owen to them and their heirs for over. As to my personal estate I leave it to the discretion of my executors." Owen died sometime between this date and July 22, "trusting and not doubting the resurrection to eternal life."[24]

On April 24, 1770, "An inventory and appointment of the estate of the Reverend Mr. Gorowny Owen, deceased" was taken. I am sobered to learn that among the "inventory" is "A negro named Peg Old" (valued at 12 pounds, 10 shillings), A negro wench named Young Peg" (40 pounds), "A do boy, Bob" (30 pounds), and "A do boy, Stephen" (15 pounds). Various pieces of furniture are noted as are assorted plates and utensils. A cow and a yearling, two heifers, one grey mare, and one grey horse are also among the effects. Twenty-five books are specifically identified by title, and valued at a little more than three pounds is "a parcel of old authors, Greek, Latin, Hebrew, Welch [sic], and French, in number, 150." Indeed it does appear that Owen did have "a comfortable home, his horse, and his negroes."[25]

23. Ibid., 162.
24. Ibid., 162.
25. Ibid., 163–64.

Goronwy and Me

Further meanderings on the Internet refer me to an article in the autumn, 1959 issue of *Virginia Cavalcade*, published quarterly by the Virginia State Library. While I could not access "Goronwy Owen: A Welsh Bard in Virginia" on-line, for a small fee I am able to procure a hard copy of the magazine. This issue also features a profile of Shirley Plantation, an account of John Brown's raid at Harper's Ferry in 1859, and the history of the honor society Phi Beta Kappa, founded in 1776 at Raleigh Tavern in Williamsburg. The piece on Goronwy Owen is by Edwin T. Williams, the rector of St. Andrew's in Lawrenceville. Mr. Williams provides a brief biographical overview of Owen's life in Wales and England emphasizing his perpetual financial difficulties. Williams writes,

> Perhaps Goronwy Owen's lot was harder than that of many other curates of his time, but it would be hard to justify. Nor will poverty justify, on the other side of the ledger, some of the difficulties into which Owen fell because of his lack of business acumen, sharp tongue, quick temper, continual borrowing and, occasionally, drinking too much. Unhappily, most writers have emphasized these shortcomings, although there is ample evidence that, along with his attainments in scholarship, he was a good pastor of his people, a prodigious worker, but very modest, a genial and kindly person with a ready wit.[26]

Mr. Williams then details the circumstances of Owen's life "in the frontier county of Brunswick, as the rector of St. Andrew's parish." According to Williams, "St. Andrew's parish covered the northern half of Brunswick County which, in 1760, contained many of the characteristics of the frontier. It was about 30 miles long by 20 miles wide and, if the method of estimating the population at three times the number of tithables be accepted, its inhabitants numbered approximately 5,247 in 1760 and 6,579 in 1769. Lawrenceville was in its infancy as a town and the vestry met in the courthouse in another part of the parish until the new middle church was completed in 1766."[27]

Mr. Williams goes on to note that the revival in Cymric literature in the first half of the 19th century and an inquiry to the Diocese of Southern Virginia in 1850 from the Cymmrodorion Society regarding information and possible manuscripts that might have survived Owen. In 1913, the author tells us, a descendant of Owen's came to Lawrenceville in search of the

---

26. Williams, "Welsh Bard," 44.
27. Ibid., 45.

poet's grave. He was assisted in this effort by Arthur Gray, then rector of St. Andrew's who published an article in the *William and Mary Quarterly* on their endeavor.

Mr. Williams reports that in 1957 he appealed to the Association for the Preservation of Virginia Antiquities to place a monument to Owen in Brunswick County. He likewise entreated the Poetry Society of Virginia who sponsored a general solicitation among its members and among the Welsh people of the United States and Canada. On March 2, 1958 a Celtic cross commemorating Owen was dedicated in the churchyard in St. Andrew's. The design for the cross came from Anglesey, Owen's place of birth through Canon Selwyn Gummer.

"And at last," Mr. Williams concludes, "the people of Great Britain, through the Honorable Society of Cymmrodorion, and the people of North America, through the Poetry Society of Virginia, have joined forces to revive and preserve the memory of the great Welsh poet who lived in Virginia."[28]

---

28. Ibid., 46.

4

Goronwy Considered

FROM CYWYDD Y FARN FAWR (CYWYDD ON THE DAY OF JUDGMENT)
by Goronwy Owen

> Enter your rightful inheritance, loving children of heaven. There bliss awaits you beyond the power of all but the pure to conceive: a pleasant privileged home peopled by saints numberless as the stars. I, in my infinite love, suffered wounds to ensure our everlasting sojourn in a world free of peril and pain.

Goronwy Considered

EVERY CHRISTMAS MORNING, SUSIE, Elise, and I gather in the living room to open the presents accumulated under the tree. We drink coffee, exclaim, "What could it be?" and gently dissuade our dog Bobby from sniffing every item. Now nineteen, Elise's gifts have evolved form American Girl Dolls (and their limitless supply of accessories) to guitars and electronics to accoutrements necessary for independent life in college. Books have always been staple gifts for Susie and me. We typically exchange one or more anticipated contemporary novels or some work of general non-fiction. Christmas, 2009, was no exception, and as I unfolded the familiarly shaped package ensconced in Susie's taut wrapping, I was pleasantly surprised to find two books. These leather bound tomes with gilt-edged pages bore the rather foreboding title, *The Poetical Works of the Rev. Goronwy Owen (Goronwy Ddu o Fon) With His Life and Correspondence.* Edited, With Notes Critical and Explanatory, by the Rev. Robert Jones, B.A., Vicar of all Saints, Rotherhitte. In Two Volumes.

Susie had acquired these "scarce" books, published in London in 1876 by Longmans, Green & Co., from an antiquarian book dealer in England. Stamped on the front page of each volume is "From the Library of the Late Revd. Owen Thomas, D.O. Liverpool. Purchased and Presented by Mr. William Thomas, Boothe, Liverpool. To the Theological College, Bala. December, 1891." It seems my healthy curiosity with Owen had officially blossomed into addiction with Susie enabling my habit! In time, I was to learn that Jones's work was the definitive study of Owen for over a century and the primary source for most Owen "scholars."

During the remaining days of Christmas break, I thumbed through the volumes, and, particularly, hunted up the description of Owen's life in Brunswick. However, I did not actually "read" the books until February when I managed to take breaks from shoveling our driveway from an unprecedented two-foot snowfall and an unscheduled holiday week from school. In the preceding sentence, read is in quotation marks because while I pored over every word, much of Jones's work is in Welsh. Understandably, Jones quotes extensively form the writings of Owen and his contemporaries who, in their letters, propagated the annoying (to me) habit of switching randomly from English to Welsh, often within the same sentence. I never could decipher a pattern or reason for these transliterations, but they occur frequently and without warning. And while Jones's work contains copious notes and translation, much of the prose is inaccessible to those unfamiliar with the Welsh tongue.

Goronwy and Me

Volume I of *The Poetical Works of the Rev. Goronwy Owen* contains, in Welsh, all of Owen's surviving poems. Attached to each are exhaustive notes. Consider, for example, Jones's introduction to "Cywydd y Farn Fawr":

> The notes appended to the poem in the previous editions were originally written by its author, but altered and multiplied to such an extent by Lewis Morris, as to warrant former editors in ascribing them altogether to the latter. His initials are consequently, appended to them.
>
> Modified, as are some of the opinions they offer, by the more enlightened philology of the present day, we yet retain them, not only as literary curiosities, but as the productions of two celebrated writers. This is said of some of them only. Others are retained for their intrinsic excellence. They exhibit a literary acumen worthy of any age.
>
> "The 'Introduction' was undoubtedly written by Lewis Morris, in the form of a letter, addressed to 'The President of the Society of Cymmrodorion in London'; and is as follows:—"[1]

Indeed the letter does follow and in the course of several pages, Morris unabashedly extols the virtues of both the poem and its poet. He alternately refers to the work as "a perfect poem," an "excellent piece" that "doth not, in my opinion, come short of anything I have hitherto met in our language." The subject of the poem is the last Day of Judgment and Morris compares and contrasts this work with Milton's *Paradise Regained* and the efforts of Homer and Virgil.

In Jones's book, "Cywydd Y Farn Fawr" covers eighteen pages with anywhere from four to sixteen lines per page. In all there are seventy-eight footnotes, and several references are in Greek, Latin, or Hebrew. Alas, the poem itself does not appear in English, and I have had to seek in other places "translations" of this and others of Owen's poems.

Volume II of *The Poetical Works of the Rev. Goronwy Owen* provides a chronological accounting of Owen's life in thirty-two chapters. This book is steeped in the minutiae of Owen's life, and as we will see, Jones is unapologetic in his praise of the poet.

Jones begins this volume with a brief introduction to the Welsh poetic tradition:

> "The Celtic family of languages, and more especially the Cymric branch, abounds in poetry. Nor is it difficult to account for this. The Celt is

---

1. Jones, *Poetical Works (Vol. II)*, 21.

of a highly poetical temperament, while his language is replete with word-painting. Instrument and agent are thus peculiarly adapted for the purposes of song. We need not wonder then, that the literature of the Welsh is rich in this species of mental production."[2]

As mentioned, Volume II is a chronological accounting of Owen's life and relies heavily on his prolific correspondence. Jones traverses Owen's boyhood rather quickly and focuses on the perpetual frustrations Owen experiences trying to earn a living while following his muse. The book is stuffed with asides and insights, as in the following:

> We have scarcely touched on Goronwy's personal appearance; but we are now called upon to do so. His frame was short and slender, but firm and wiry, supple too and lithesome as an ash plant. Had the gymnasium been then in vogue, he would have excelled in athletic exercises. As it was, he could leap to an extraordinary distance, or walk fifty miles at a stretch. He was of a dark complexion; his hair and beard were quite black—the latter, even when closely shaven, peering out from his lip and chin. The eye, however, was his most remarkable feature. The dark hue burst into light and fire under the influence of emotion. We have spoken of his quickness of temper; not a whit less quick was the lightning flash his eye emitted, when moved by either pleasure or anger.[3]

Jones makes clear throughout the book Owen's affection for his native language. In a 1754 letter to Richard Morris, Owen writes, "The more I know of the Welsh language, the more I love and admire it; and think in my heart, if we had some men of genius and abilities of my way of thinking, we should have not need to despair of seeing it in a flourishing a condition as any other, ancient or modern."[4]

This estimation is echoed in another letter to Richard Morris who had implored Owen to write an ode to the Prince of Wales. Owen begins,

> Dear Sir, —Nothing could have been more agreeable to me than to employ my Muse on the subject you sent me. But the more agreeable the subject, the more I regret the vast inequality of my poor muse to such and arduous task. If, therefore, it is not so well executed as I could wish, I readily own it is owing to my own incapacity, and not to any defect in our language. For that is—at least I am willing to believe it is—adequate to the highest strains of

2. Ibid., 1.
3. Ibid., 66.
4. Ibid., 146–47.

> panegyric, and abundantly fitted by copiousness and significancy to express the sublimest thoughts, and in as sublime a manner as any other language is capable of reaching to.[5]

Ever Owen's cheerleader, Jones applauds the poet's gift and control of his mother tongue:

> We have often marveled, and we marvel still, at Goronwy's mastery of the Welsh language. Whence came it? The only books he was acquainted with in his early years were the Bible and *Y Bardd Cwsg*—models the most pure, it is true, but circumscribed in their range and of a comparatively recent date; while Goronwy's vocabulary, even if deprived of the thousands of words contained in both, would be a rich and extensive one. We again wonderingly ask, Whence did he derive his knowledge? It could not have been at Oswestry, or Donnington, or Walton. Yet he, an exile from Wales, a resident for years in the heart of England, not only wrote gracefully and graphically in Welsh, but proved himself a more consummate master of it, both etymologically and idiomatically, than any writer either of that or any succeeding age. We can ascribe it to nothing less than a genius as transcendent as was ever bestowed on man. Our English readers may perhaps smile at our enthusiasm, and deem it an exaggeration; but were they acquainted with our Cymric language, they would, we are satisfied, endorse our opinion, nor fancy we had said too much.[6]

Given his almost atavistic love of his native language, Owen feared his children would never "learn Welsh to any perfection." None of his children ever lived in Wales, so his fear was undoubtedly justified and realized.

Regarding his own work, Owen maintained, "Whatever I have written was designed for men, and for men of sense and ingenuity, such as love their country and language, and can relish pithy and nervous Welsh. As for those squeamish stomachs that can digest nothing without English sauce, I would direct them to Wil Goch y Sign, or Evan Ellis, where, for the value of a single penny, they may be supplied with the gibberish a la mode of the best and most rhyme-taggers of the age."[7]

---

5. Ibid., 52.
6. Ibid., 123–24.
7. Ibid., 191.

Elsewhere, Owen insists that he does not write for critics, "but for rational creatures-for such, I mean, as have sense enough to form a right judgement of things, and candour enough to pass an impartial one."[8]

Jones takes pains to point out that Owen was more than the master of poetry. Near the end of the book, Jones writes that "the excellence of Goronwy's style of Welsh prose-writing . . . has never been surpassed, we are sure; we doubt that it has ever been equaled." Jones then comments on the grace and elegance of one of Owen's letters, and concludes, "It is deeply to be regretted, we again say, that no great work [of prose] was consummated by the poet. It would have become a text-book in our language, and a model for future writers; for if the thoughts and small indication of hastily penned letters are thus happy, what excellence, we may gather, would be found I his more carefully prepared compositions!"[9]

At one point in his work, Jones comments that,

> biography, to be of interest, should record not only the leading incidents of a life, but its details. Our impressions of character are formed more from the little circumstances—the minutiae—of every day, than from any extraordinary or unusual events that interfere with its course. The windings of a river are discernible only when its waters run within their channel, not when summer suns have dried up or wintry floods have swollen and spread them far and wide over the landscape. The landmarks are then lost.[10]

Jones does examine the "minutiae" of Owen's life and writes frankly, if apologetically, about the poet's struggles with alcohol. As Jones says, "It is with no feigned sorrow that we record these failings of our poet. We would gladly pass them by were not truth at stake. A biography that records the virtues only of the characters it depicts, concealing or glossing over their blemishes, is not an honest one." According to Jones, "while [Owen] inherited the many excellent qualities of his mother, the incomparable Siân Parri, he succeeded to much of the unstable, erratic disposition of his father, Owen Gorowny."[11]

Owen apparently experienced prolonged and intense episodes of drinking, especially on visits to Liverpool where,

---

8. Ibid., 82.
9. Ibid., 242–43.
10. Ibid., 224–25.
11. Ibid., 85–86.

> We are afraid that the allurements of which we have spoken a few pages back [alcohol], had already begun to make inroads on his nobler life. And how easily are these untoward habits formed! And when formed, with what difficulty are they overcome! We sometimes speak of them as cords that bind a strong man; but cords may be snapped or unstranded. In their true character, and as all experience proves, they are manacles of iron, which a giant's strength can neither burst nor unrivet. Alas! for our poor bard with his pliant and social temperament![12]

Wow, easy on the exclamation marks, Mr. Jones!

As an acquaintance instructed one looking for Owen in Liverpool, "go to a certain low street in the lowest quarter of the town, and when there go to the lowest public house, [where] you will find Goronwy seated in the chimney corner of the kitchen." As Jones reasons, "We can but wonder at the narrow space that divides the loftiness from the littleness of our nature."[13]

Jones concludes,

> But we cannot quit the subject without reiterating the extenuating circumstances which the poet's life present us. If for the moment he forgot the claims of his social position as a clergyman, it must be remembered that he had been ignored by the bishops, driven into exile from all that was dear to him, and consigned to a life of servitude with no adequate remuneration for his labors, either as a minister or a schoolmaster. In addition, and more grievous than all, the vice of intemperance, in the person of his wife, was not only destroying his present comfort, but wrecking his hopes for the future. In such a nursery, how were his children to be brought up?[14]

It was at this nadir in his life that "his little daughter—the Elin over whose birth he had rejoiced some seventeen months before, and who in the interval had been a bright sunbeam gladdening his home, fell a victim to the complaint he had himself so acutely suffered. She died after but a few days' illness, and was buried within two or three paces of the spot that witnessed her birth." Jones goes on to say that Elin's death "almost prostrated

---

12. Ibid., 127.
13. Ibid., 180.
14. Ibid., 182–83.

the poor father" who "poured forth his wailings in an ode of exquisite pathos."[15] Owen's "Elegy for His Daughter Ellen" appears below:

> Too sad is the grief in my heart! Down my cheeks run salt streams. I have lost my Ellen of the hue of fair weather, my bright-braided merry daughter.
>
> My darling, bright-shaped, beautiful, my warm-smiling angel; a golden speech was the infant talk of her lips, the girl of the colour of the stars (what profit now to speak?), whose form was delicate, whose voice was soft, with a happy cry to welcome her father, that orphaned man. Orphaned is her father, with a crushing wound in his pierced and broken heart, in inconsolable distress- how well I know, bound down with my yearning for her!
>
> Since I lost my neat slender girl, all the time I mourn her sadly and ponder on her ways. When I think of her, anguish springs up and wretched affliction in my breast, my heart is faint for her and broken because of her; it is a pang to speak of her, try trim daughter, of the dear gentle words she uttered, and of her delicate pale white hands.
>
> Farewell, my soul, my joyful gay princess, farewell again, my Nelly, pure of heart, farewell my pretty little merry daughter, my angel, resting in the midst of the graveyard at Walton, until the far assembly of the white Saints and the cry of the clamour of the unfailing Messenger. When the earth shall give up its meek and innocent, when the throngs shall be summoned for the mighty oceans, you shall get, my soul, you too, a fine gold crown and a place in the light of the host of angels.

It is little wonder, perhaps, that two years after Ellen's death, "Goronwy's sojourn . . . in England, came to an end. In vain has search been made for the immediate cause of his leaving. There is no light to be thrown on it. It may be assumed that the tempting of so large an income as £200 per annum to a man in the deepest poverty induced him to quit his native shore for the distant one." As previously noted, Owen appealed to the members of the Cymmrodorion Society for help in defraying the expense of the relocation, and as his ship left London and "glided down the broad stream, his thoughts, like waters that had been temporarily dammed up, at length broke loose and overwhelmed him with their forebodings. Should he ever return? He was leaving behind him, not only the home of his boyhood and the coveted retreat of his riper years, but the shores of one world to step out an exile and friendless on those of another." Not only that, Jones writes, but

15. Ibid., 203.

his "fellow passengers were a motley crew, a herd swept out of society, as mud is swept out of the streets, to be borne away where they could contaminate English homes no more."[16]

When Owen arrived in Williamsburg in 1758—having lost his wife and youngest son during the voyage—he assumed his position as Master of the grammar school connected with the College of William and Mary. As Jones reports, "Little is known of [Owen's] life during the three years he remained in Williamsburg." But, Jones acknowledges, "One or two circumstances, however, boom prominently out of the darkness with which these years are enveloped. Gorowny . . . wooed and won Mrs. Clayton, a widow, Dame of the College, and sister of the Reverend Thomas Dawson, its President." Jones concludes, "The union speaks well for the poet's address and person. What else had he to recommend him? Nothing; except his poverty and the 'incumbrance' of two boys." However, "Goronwy's new happiness . . . was but short-lived. The wife he had married, and who seemed destined to transform his wretched home into a scene of comfort, died within a year of their union."[17]

Jones speculates that after his wife's death, Owen reverted to "grosser habits," and, as we know, in 1760, Owen resigned his position after leading the boys of the College in a fray with the young men of the town. Jones believes Owen's intemperance also contributed to his banishment, for "familiar as we are with the 'gown and town rows' of our two great Universities, and deprecating such unseemly contests, still we doubt if they were the sole cause of the breaking up of Goronwy's connexion with the college."[18]

Jones concludes this chapter—Chapter XXX—in the following manner:

> "Alas poor Bard! There is yet one more scene into which we must follow thee—the closing scene. That done, we shall bid thee farewell and leave thee in thy nameless, unknown grave; but not to be forgotten there. Thy memory is embalmed in our heart, and in every true Cymric heart, for ever!"[19]

The closing scene, of course, is set in Brunswick County. Jones writes, "Of Goronwy's life at St. Andrew's there is nothing to record beyond the death of his son, and his marriage, for the third time, with a wife by whom he had three children. Despite diligent search, we have been unable

16. Ibid., 273–74.
17. Ibid., 283–84.
18. Ibid., 291.
19. Ibid.

to discover any account of his home, or of his parish, or of his new life-partner. In fact, St. Andrew's itself is scarcely recognizable in either map or gazetteer." Furthermore, Jones concludes, "Remote as Williamsburg was from the scenes and associations so dear to Goronwy, St. Andrew's was still more so. Not only was its population sparse, but it must have been an illiterate one."[20]

"Still," Jones maintains, "the Welsh language sparkled form [Owen's] lips and pen as fluently as ever. The Awdl to which allusion has been made [An Elegy to Lewis Morris] was written after an absence from Wales of nearly twenty years. Not only is it a marvelous literary feat in its enunciation of thought, but it is also a master-piece of Cymric expression. Its cynghannedd—that 'concord of sweet sounds,' has never been surpassed."[21]

In the last chapter of his work, Jones traces the revival of interest in Owen's work since his death more than a century ago, and he assesses, "Wherever the Welsh language is spoken, there also the creations of his pen are read and valued for their classic beauty, their originality, and freshness." Jones brings his book to its conclusion by writing, "In retracing their [Owen and the Morris brothers] footsteps over life's weary road, we have so frequently shared their sorrows and their joys, that now the journey is ended, it is almost with tears that we bid them a last farewell."[22]

I really enjoyed my reading of *The Poetical Works of the Rev. Goronwy Owen* despite my complete and utter inability to glean any insight into the Welsh language. Jones's book is original, and I admire the fact that the author is such an unrepentant advocate for his subject. Sure, the language is full of hyperbole, but there is a rhythm and a felicity of phrasing I find engaging. And there seems to be no question concerning Jones's scholarship—his knowledge of Owen is exhaustive. I say, "Hats off to you, the Reverend Mr. Jones!" (Notice the exclamation mark.)

Goronwy Owen by Branwen Jarvis offers a stark contrast to the Reverend Jones's biography. Published in 1986 by the University of Wales Press, it is an honest and measured examination of the poet's life. Only eighty-five pages, Goronwy Owen examines the "major irony which underlies Goronwy's work," the "duality that exists" between Owen's poetry and, through

---

20. Ibid., 293.
21. Ibid., 296.
22. Ibid., 301.

his letters, his prose. As Jarvis points out, Owen's poems reflect "clarity, precision, and elegance," while his letters are full of "rumbustiousness."[23]

This dichotomy, Jarvis asserts, illustrates that for Owen, "the reality and the dream were tragically far apart."

Jarvis's booklet examines various periods of Owen's life and the poems produced during each of these phases. She goes on to explore the poet's philosophy regarding his work and the disparate influences on his writing. Jarvis also examines Owen's skill as a writer of prose, and, finally she considers the nature of his reputation today.

Jarvis points out that as a young man, Owen received a thorough education, despite the financial limitations of his family. As he wrote in a letter appealing for funds to attend Oxford or Cambridge,

> By the unwearied industry of my parents, who are exceedingly poor, I was enabled to attend the public school at Bangor, from the year 1737 to 1741. At this time, I had reached the limit proposed to me there, and gone through the studies of the School; and then returned to my parents. My mother being dead, and my father married to another wife, I was left to struggle on alone. Unaccustomed to labour, I see before no means of getting a livelihood, and learning is but an additional light, by which I discern more clearly the wretchedness before me. [24]

Owen did go to Oxford in the summer of 1742, but according to Jarvis, he stayed for only one week, thus ending his formal education. He took a position as an usher, a type of apprentice schoolmaster, at the Grammar School in Pwllheli and left in 1744 after two years service. He went next to Denbigh Grammar School in 1745, again as an usher, but in January, 1746, he was ordained a deacon at Bangor and sent to his native parish as a curate. He was not long in this position as the Bishop replaced Owen with "a young clergyman of a very great fortune."[25]

After a brief hiatus in Denbigh, Owen removed to a curacy in Owestry in Shropshire and, excepting one trip when he was ordained a priest, never again set foot in Wales. In 1747, Owen married Elin Hughes, and his home permanently assumed the character of an English home. At Oswestry in 1748, Owen was arrested for debt and trespass, thus beginning, as Jarvis suggests, a pattern of Owen's "seeming inability to manage the practical

23. Jarvis, *Goronwy Owen*, 1.
24. Ibid., 5.
25. Ibid., 10.

realities of life."²⁶ It was at this time that Owen, through the encouragement of Lewis Morris, resolved to compose poetry.

Owen and his young family moved to Donnington and there, according to Jarvis, he wrote "many of his best-known poems ... within a period of fifteen months or so between 1752 and 1754." Yet, also during this time, as Jarvis insists, Owen demonstrated that he "possessed little gift for harmonious friendship."²⁷ His "contrariness" at times alienated him from the Morris brothers, who seemed unstinting in their efforts to help him.

The Owen family next settled in Walton, near Liverpool. It was here, in April, 1755, that his daughter Elin died and where he composed his elegy for her. This poem, Jarvis writes, "is highly conventional, stylized even, but it is a heartfelt expression of a father's grief, all the more moving for its dignity and lack of hysteria." Still, Jarvis concludes, "it is a poem that has one dimension only, the general; whereas the best poetry of this kind is a fusion of several dimensions."²⁸ Apparently in Walton, Owen enjoyed improved material comfort, but his sense of isolation was strong.

In May of 1755, at the invitation of the Cymmrodorion Society, Owen relocated to London, and within a few months he was placed in a curacy in Northolt, just north of the city. Though his living here was "reasonably comfortable," Jarvis maintains that,

> Nowhere are the ironic sadnesses in Goronwy's life and work more apparent than in the poems of the Northolt period ... It was at Northolt that he gave his feelings for Môn [Anglesey] their finest and most poignant expression. The major irony of his life, that his love and longing were to be ever unrequited, was daily becoming more apparent. This love and longing is manifested in Cywydd in Praise for Anglesey.²⁹

According to Jarvis,

> From start to finish, the poem recognizes the supremacy of God's will: all, ultimately, is in God's hand and Goronwy accepts unquestioningly God's design for him. It is this conviction which gives the poem its wide and long perspective. Goronwy's longing for Môn, seen in the light of God's eternity, fades in its significance, and, therefore, in its capacity to cause pain. The poem's final passages

---

26. Ibid., 12.
27. Ibid., 18.
28. Ibid., 22.
29. Ibid., 31–32.

are suffused with a sense of the deep tranquility which Goronwy had gained, not by disregarding earth's pain and responsibilities, but by meditating upon them in terms of life everlasting.[30]

It was during his tenure at Northolt that Owen temporarily severed his relationship with Lewis Morris. Jarvis writes, "We do not know the direct cause of Goronwy Owen's quarrel with Lewis Morris; it may be Lewis's generosity, as well as his patience, had been strained to the breaking point by Goronwy's demands, and that he refused to supply him with more money." Whatever the cause for the break, Goronwy responded by penning a poem in which he viciously attacks Morris, calling him a "witless oaf," a "half-breed between man and devil" whose "supreme god was ruddy gold and a fistful of gold was his soul." Understandably, according to Morris's nephew, Lewis "can never stand any mention of poor Goronwy, Goronwy's work is like dirt nowadays."[31]

Shortly after this breech, Owen accepted the position in Williamsburg, and, according to Jarvis, "Goronwy the writer did not, in any significant way, survive the journey to America."[32] (Jarvis's claim is countermanded by Hywel M. Davies in his article "Goronwy Owen, the Parsons' Cause and The College of William and Mary in Virginia." Davies concludes his piece by asserting, "Amongst the woods and fields of his tobacco plantation, he [Owen] wrote a masterful, classical, and traditional Marwnad to his erstwhile mentor, Lewis Morris. Goronwy Owen's Muse, which his friends feared would canker and fester through disuse in America, found its glorious voice in the Virginia Southside. His living at St. Andrew's parish, in both senses, liberated him from the distraction of others and did not inhibit the genius which produced in the Marwnad the finest Welsh poetry to be composed outside the British Isles.[33]) Jarvis touches briefly on Owen's years in America and concludes,

> The story of Goronwy's life, through all its vicissitudes from its beginnings at Rhos-fawr to its premature end on a Virginia plantation is sadder, stormier, more dramatic than any story a novelist would dare to create. Inevitably, such a history works upon the feelings and the imagination. Goronwy Owen has generated powerful reactions among succeeding generations of readers, and

30. Ibid., 35–36.
31. Ibid., 39–41.
32. Ibid., 44.
33. Davies, "Parsons' Cause," 64.

those reactions frequently have as much to do with Goronwy the man as with Goronwy the writer.³⁴

Jarvis departs from the biographical strand of her study to look at the influences on Owen's poetry and his philosophy of composition. As she points out, "Owen was heir to several classicisms," including the Welsh tradition of strict-meter poetry, the influences of Greek and Roman literature, the ideas of the Renaissance, and the poetry of Milton. In general, "Goronwy Owen eschews fact in favour of hyperbole, claiming that sublimity of imagination leads one to a higher truth than the merely factual." Furthermore, "too great an insistence on detail is inimical to a wide-ranging and imaginative response."³⁵

Jarvis goes on to assert that, "For Goronwy true poetry was, and always had been, exclusively the province of men of learning." Furthermore, he insisted that, "the language of poetry should be the language of men of learning and culture." Jarvis traces Owen's affection of the Welsh language and the congruence of feeling between the eighteenth century of Owen's life and the "Golden Age" of Welsh poetry three centuries earlier. Jarvis acknowledges, "The truth is that it was in metrical matters, that he followed Welsh tradition." However, she continues, "In matters of style, he owes as much to his own time as to the strict-metre poets of the past" and "in matters of content . . . there is no doubt where Goronwy Owen belongs: it is to his own time."³⁶

Finally, "For Goronwy Owen . . . happiness was to be found only in God." Jarvis writes that, "he believed all poetry is divinely inspired" and that his "attitude to his role as a poet is governed by his [religious] conviction. He approaches the role with the same committed seriousness that we saw in his approach to the role of a priest."³⁷

Jarvis next looks at the style of Owen's prose, sharply contrasting it with the "sacred nature" of his poetry. As Jarvis points out, "His letters are unfettered by any idea of high calling. His poems are restricted, restrained, disciplined by the calls of tradition and artistry and an elevated view of the subject-matter of poetry. With his letters, though they too have literary antecedents, we are in a world which is altogether freer and less hidebound." Jarvis insists that, "the most colorful and extravagant passages in Goronwy's

---

34. Jarvis, *Goronwy Owen*, 46–47.
35. Ibid., 48–51.
36. Ibid., 55–61
37. Ibid., 67–69.

letters occur when he is writing in satiric vein," the best example of which is his letter to Richard Morris from aboard the *Trial*.[38]

In general, Owen's letters vary greatly in their subject matter and their prose style:

> He can be racy and vigorous when occasion demands, while at other times he writes with scriptural formality and grace. He can write of everyday events in narrative of commendable directness and simplicity, and then turn, in the very next sentence, to discussing problems of criticism with clarity and elegance. He can write of Anglesey or of his children affectingly and unsentimentally. And, almost always, the letters are lively and immensely readable. The charge of dullness has been levied against some of his poems. Such a charge against his letters is inconceivable.[39]

The last chapter of Jarvis's book explores the "literary hero-worship" of Owen. She concludes that, "the passionate admiration of the nineteenth century re-emerged in the early years of the twentieth as a considered and scholarly appraisal which still accorded his work very high praise."[40]

Jarvis offers her own assessment in the book's final paragraph:

> It seems to me that we do Goronwy's name a disservice by concentrating too much of our attention on his fairly limited poetic output, to the exclusion of other aspects of his work and influence. Goronwy Owen was more than a poet. He was an accomplished and versatile writer of prose and an astute critic in linguistic and literary matters. In historical terms, he is a figure of great importance. He revitalized a decaying poetic tradition and assured its survival. It has been the object of this study to give due weight to these several aspects, in the hope that, taken together, they may make a realistic appraisal of Goronwy Owen possible.[41]

In my mind, Jarvis does provide a "realistic appraisal" of Owen. Her book is informative and measured, certainly more of an even-handed examination than the one offered by the Rev. Jones. Reading these two books has educated me on the poet's life and work, but I feel there is more to learn. Particularly, I wonder if there exists more information on Owen's life

---

38. Ibid., 70–73.
39. Ibid., 77.
40. Ibid., 83.
41. Ibid., 84–85.

in Brunswick. Also, I'm curious to know more about the dedication of the monument at St. Andrew's, which, after all, occurred in my lifetime.

5

Goronwy Celebrated

**FROM CYWYDD ARWYRAIN Y NENAWR
(THE GARRET POEM)**
by Goronwy Owen

    And the fine extent of all my wealth
    Is the light of day, and a wise book . . . A very full mind of two kinds,
    A constant memory, and an empty purse,
    A place for my head under the eaves,
    Of some sort, thrice six yards above ground.

Goronwy Celebrated

IN THEIR RESPECTIVE BIOGRAPHIES of Owen, both Jones and Jarvis write extensively about the Cymmrodorion Society, which was instrumental in encouraging and sustaining the exiled poet. I look up the society on the internet and discover it still exists and that, furthermore, I can become a member of this venerable institution. Why not? I fill out the requested information, give credit card particulars for the twenty dollar membership, and press "send." I soon receive the following reply from Ken Kyffin, Membership Secretary:

> Dear Proal,
>
> Welcome to the Cymmrodorion. Your name has been added to the membership list and you should shortly be getting a copy of the latest transactions—these are actually $15 and cover the lectures and activities of 2008; we are very late publishing this year.
>
> As far as your subscription is concerned we owe you a most abject apology. Although the web page states clearly the rate is $20, you will find that about $31.80 has been paid from your account. This is entirely our fault and if you so wish we will refund the difference. The current website is scheduled for a rebuild as quite a few embarrassing errors and inconsistencies have found their way onto it. However the corrected site will show that our new subscription rates for overseas members from 1st Jan 2010 is £30 (GBP) which at today's exchange rate is $47.71. Looked at in this light it might be argued that you could be getting a bargain. Nonetheless the offer of a refund still stands because our system is grossly at fault.

I respond to Ken (we are on a first-name basis, after all) assuring him that there is no need for a refund. I also remark that "I first became interested in the Cymmrodorion while researching Goronwy Owen, the 18th century Welsh poet and clergyman who died in Brunswick County, Virginia, the home of my youth."

Ken replies immediately:

> Dear Proal,
>
> I'm glad to hear that we don't have to find a way of paying for our sins. Thank you for that.
>
> The requested article [one of the perks of membership] is attached. Apologies for the quality, if time had permitted I could have done better. For interest I've added the front cover of Alan Llwyd's 1997 book (in Welsh) on Goronwy, the most comprehensive work to date. It came in useful to keep the lid down while scanning

so that the ambient light only effected page 1. Alan also started work on a film script but money was not forthcoming despite the fact that a previous film he scripted about a much less interesting welsh poet was highly successful even receiving an Oscar nomination. Even after 250 years, Gronwy Ddu's shadow still hangs heavy over us.

Llwyd's biography of Owen is titled *Gronwy Ddiafael, Gronwy Ddu: Cofiant Goronwy Owen 1723–1769*, and the facsimile of the cover Ken sent me is simply amazing. The bottom third of the illustration depicts a bucolic rural village with tidy white houses and several trim, steeple-topped churches. Traveling up the book jacket, the eye gazes upon a scene of urban depredation and wantonness. The center of the scene shows a slatternly, bare-breasted, seemingly intoxicated woman dressed in rags propped upon a set of stairs. A startled infant is falling from her arms to an unseen street (canal?) below. In the background, a man and a dog gnaw on a bone and a corpse is lowered into a coffin. On one side of the illustration there appears to be an altercation going on, above which one can detect through a crumbled wall the image of a man hanging from a rafter. This whole scene is hellish and, I wonder, if it's meant to suggest the dichotomy between the idealized and the real in Owen's life. Perhaps the book's cover mirrors Owen's exile from his beloved Anglesey to the lurid enticements of Liverpool and London. Hmmm.

The "requested article" Ken forwarded me is "A Concise History of the Society 1751–1951" by Professor Emrys Jones, FBA. A footnote reveals that this article is based on "The History of the Honourable Society of Cymmrodorion 1751–1951" by R. T. Jenkins and Helen M. Ramage published in Volume L of *Y Cymmrodor*. In the article, Professor Jones writes that the Society's "genius is in part the story of the brothers Morris of Anglesey." According to Jones, Richard Morris (1702–78), 'Father of the Cymmrodorion,' "came to London in 1721, and was truly a London Welshman for fifty-seven years, returning to Anglesey once only."

Jones continues,

> But the outstanding genius in the Morris family was Lewis (1701–1765). He began life as a surveyor in Anglesey, and was commissioned to survey the coasts of Wales, a work which was published in 1748. Later he became involved in mining in Cardiganshire. He spent several long periods in London, in 1753, 1754, 1755 and 1756–58, and certainly enlivened the new society with his mercurial personality. William, Richard, and Lewis had

an intense interest in poetry, in particular the 'strict' measures, so in addition to 'classical' output they were collectors of traditional verse, transcript volumes of which are now in the British Library, and were determined to rehabilitate the Welsh language. Their interests were paramount to the programme of the Cymmrodorion Society, and it was Lewis Morris' authority that gave the Society its status in Wales, while Richard's enthusiasm generated its success in London.[1]

There is little mention of Owen in the history. Nonetheless, despite the fact that I have not a drop of Welsh blood in my veins, I am delighted to be a member of such an august institution, one that counts Goronwy Owen among its "men of letters."

One day in early 2010, I'm walking on the Downtown Mall, when I run into Kate, a friend from church who teaches history at Mary Baldwin College in Staunton. We chat about our respective children and the state of church politics. (We had served on the Vestry together.) Kate is from Scotland, so I naturally ask her, "Do you know anyone who speaks Welsh?" (I know, but it's how my mind works.) She asks why, and I give her the two-minute version of Goronwy Owen's life and what has become my "project." I explain to her the frustrations involved in trying to make sense of frequently encountered words such as "cywydd." Basically, I tell her, I'd like to know what this and other terms sound like so I may have a sense of the language when I read these words. In fact, Kate has a colleague at the college from Wales who teaches philosophy and religious studies. And, get this: his name is Roderic Owen! Kate says she will email Roderic and explain who I am and what my interest is.

She does so, and I follow up with Roderic requesting a time to get together so I might ask him some basic questions about Wales, its history, and its language. Roderic, himself, has an interest in Goronwy, and he graciously invites me to lunch in Staunton on a blustery day in February. From his own books, Roderic has photocopied for me some biographical information on Owen, as well as translations of a few of his poems. These are most helpful. I share with him what I know of Owen's life in Virginia and express my desire to do some writing on that life. Roderic tells me a bit of the story of his own family which seems to generally reflect the Welsh experience in the twentieth century. Roderic's father was a clergyman who moved to the United States when Roderic was a small boy. Growing up,

---

1. Jones, "Concise History," 6–7.

both Welsh and English were spoken in Roderic's household. According to Roderic, his father had two sisters. One remained in Wales and her family speaks Welsh today. The other sister married an Englishman and Welsh is never spoken in their home near Liverpool. Today, Roderic estimates that about 800,000 of Wales' three million citizens still primarily converse in their native tongue. He goes on to give me a few pronunciation hints and informs me that BBC Wales has a language primer on its website. The foreign language company Rosetta Stone also offers a Welsh language program, he says. He invites me to attend the International Conference on Welsh Studies to be held in July at Marymount University in Arlington, Virginia. My time with Roderic is indeed fruitful, and we pledge to stay in touch going forward.

In early spring, Mother sends me a photograph from March, 1958, taken at the dedication of the Goronwy Owen monument at St. Andrew's. The Celtic cross is in the foreground of this black and white picture. A small platform is behind the cross, and at the moment of this photograph, someone on the platform is speaking to the unseen crowd. Others are seated on this stage, including my father. He is at this moment thirty-eight years old, and it is refreshing to have this image of him as a young man. The day looks gray indeed and the bare branches of the trees form a spectral latticework in the background. Perhaps this is appropriate given the temperament of the man being honored.

Mother also sends me a brochure titled *The Goronwy Owen Story in the Twentieth Century in Saint Andrew's Parish*. There are twenty-one photographs with corresponding captions in this publication, the purpose of which is to "show some of those who have been concerned with the Owen story as it has touched St. Andrew's Parish." There are several pictures from the dedication ceremony and from the church service that followed. There is a photograph of David Lloyd of Brownsville, Maine, a lineal descendent of Owen, who came to Lawrenceville in 1913 to search for the poet's grave. He was assisted in this endeavor by the Reverend Arthur P. Gray (also pictured), who was the rector of St. Andrew's at the time. Both men were deceased when the monument was dedicated. According to the brochure, "the story of this search along with notes on the life of the Rev. Mr. Owen was published in Welsh (1947) by Isaac Lloyd, nephew of David Lloyd."

In 1928, the Rev. Gray published "Outline of Evidence Concerning Burial Place of Gronow Owen" in the *William and Mary Quarterly*. Prepared from notes made in 1913, this document is divided into two parts:

Goronwy Celebrated

"To show that he was buried in Brunswick County" and "To show the particular spot at which he was buried." For the first part, Gray cites reference works, a letter from one of Owen's descendents, and, most compellingly, "many county records refer to his residence there, and his will is among those records, probated March 26, 1770." Regarding the "particular spot," the Rev. Mr. Gray traces the efforts that he and Mr. Lloyd made in April or May, 1913. They learned that when Owen's son Richard sold his portion of the family estate, "he reserved a lot 12 feet square for a graveyard." Mr. Lloyd and the Rev. Gray traced the land to its present owner, "a negro by the name of Allen" who they subsequently visited. Allen took them to an old burying-ground "that had always been protected from cultivation" which was located in a "small clump of trees and tangled vines." Mr. Gray goes on to report that "some weeks after this I went with a negro to the old graveyard referred to, and we cleared away some of the tangled growth about the center of the cluster." Gray hoped to find some evidence or "solid remnants" of a burial place, "But with the means at my disposal, I was able to go only two or three inches down, over the surface we had cleared, not deep enough to reveal anything of interest that might have been there."[2]

The Rev. Gray concludes his outline "offering to assist in any way . . . in further efforts for verification." He suggests that "interested persons" thoroughly examine "pertinent Brunswick County records and that "inquiries be made of all descendents of Gronowy Owen who can be reached." He hopes that excavations of the old burying spot will be made and that, at the very least, "some inexpensive metal or stone markers be placed about this spot now" to secure the location for future investigation.[3]

The work of the Rev. Mr. Gray is referred to in an article that appeared in 1935 in *Y Cymmrodor*, "the magazine of The Honourable Society of Cymmrodorion." Written by B. B. Thomas, M. A., this piece "is an attempt to co-ordinate much evidence that is scattered in several articles" by those who have tried to improve our knowledge of Goronwy Owen's "last phase."[4] In his article, Thomas traces the political and ecclesiastical climate of "the sixties of the eighteenth century in Virginia." He goes on to profile the Brunswick County and St. Andrew's parish of that era and the circumstances leading to Owen's investiture as rector. Thomas also writes that,

2. Gray, "Outline," 213–14.
3. Ibid., 215.
4. Thomas, "Rector of St. Andrew's," 113.

> on August 20th, 1761, he [Owen] completed the deed of purchase of some four hundred acres of land from Wilham Cocke and Rebecca his wife. The price paid was £90. As this land was part of Mrs. Cocke's dowry a further deed was necessary, dated February 27th, 1762, in which, she declared that the sale was concluded "without the persuasion or threats of the said Wilham Cocke." [5]

Thomas also examines the vestry records during Owen's tenure and notes that the vestry supplemented Owen's income for "keeping and carrying to church the sacramental plate." On another occasion, Owen "was allowed £2 12s for wine for the sacrament for the year 1762–63." Thomas states that Owen was present at the vestry meeting on January 14, 1769, but

> when the vestry next met on July 22nd the Rev. Thomas Lundie was inducted into the rectory benefice and cure of the parish for Goronwy was dead. He had apparently been unwell in the early summer and had gone to Blanford about forty miles distant to stay with his brother-in-law. He wrote his wife on June 24th, 1769, asking her to join him, bringing the two youngest children with her and leaving the other two with her parents. He was then seriously ill. His will is dated July 3rd. Sometime between that date and July 22nd he died, and it is practically certain that according to colonial custom he was buried on his own plantation.[6]

Blanford is located near Petersburg which seems to suggest that Owen, in fact, did not die in Brunswick County. It is interesting to me that this tidbit of information comes from an article written in an ostensibly Welsh journal in 1935 that I found on the internet from the library of the University of Toronto.

Early in the summer of 2010, I determine to visit Brunswick County. I want to see if I can find any additional information regarding the dedication of the memorial at St. Andrew's, and, possibly, try to locate Owen's grave site. I convince Randy, a friend from church and beer-drinking buddy, to go with me. Actually, Randy, originally from Memphis, Tennessee, is interested in the excursion because his own family research has indicated that he might have "some people" from Brunswick County.

We set off early on what will be a hot, sunny day and roll into Lawrenceville after a 2½ hour drive down Interstates 64 and 85. Driving along Windsor Avenue, I show Randy my house, my grandmother's house, and

5. Ibid., 120.
6. Ibid., 120–125.

the entrance to St. Paul's College. We pull into the parking lot of St. Andrew's so I can point out to Randy the Celtic cross monument to Owen. We notice a man leaving the church, and I introduce myself to him. It's Johnny Miller, who I vaguely remember from my childhood, and who reminds me that my mother taught his wife, Bonnie Thomas, at Brunswick High School. Johnny is the junior warden of the church, which he obligingly opens for Randy and me. We look around (I show Randy the plaque in honor of my grandfather) and talk about the church, then and now. I mention to Johnny my interest in Goronwy Owen. I tell him that I had read a "blog" in which some other Owen devotee had been guided to the poet's gravesite by a man named Wayne Gilley. Johnny tells me that Mr. Gilley lives next door to the post office in Dolphin, a piece of information that proves useful later that afternoon.

We thank Johnny and proceed downtown to the Brunswick County Museum and Historical Society, housed in the former library. I learn that the museum doesn't really have any "papers" per se, but one of the docents calls the library on my behalf and learns that it does possess some files on Goronwy Owen. Randy locates a couple of books with references to his potential ancestor, and while he makes notes (no photocopier), I chat with the two elderly docents. I tell them I'm from Lawrenceville, and they remember my father. These ladies are sisters-in-law from out in the county and one, Rachel Abernathy, recalls watching her brother R. C. once play baseball against Daddy and the town boys at "Crossroads," some seven miles removed from Lawrenceville. I am flabbergasted because this is a story I know well. Not only did Daddy tell it often (as he did with most of his stories), it is also in the memoir he wrote for his children. In my mind I recall the details of this contest between "the county boys and the city slickers," including the walk from Lawrenceville to Crossroads, the gangling, fireballing opposing pitcher Flournoy, and how after the game, Mr. Abernathy treated the (losing) Lawrenceville boys to lemonade and a ride part way home in his Model A. I am somewhat stunned to meet an eyewitness to this game, which happened about eighty years ago.

Randy completes his note taking, so we thank the nice ladies and walk over to Pino's, Lawrenceville's only restaurant, for lunch. After a cheeseburger "with all the fixins'" ($2.95), fries, and sweet tea, we amble across the street to the public library which is now located in the building that once served as Lawrenceville's movie theater. The theater has been closed for about fifty years now, although I do have a vague memory of seeing

101 Dalmatians there when I was a little boy. If so, I and the other white patrons sat downstairs, while African-American moviegoers watched from the balcony, which they had entered by way of a staircase on the side of the building. It was always my understanding that the theater closed rather than fully integrate, although economics could have played a part as well.

At the circulation desk, I inquire after the materials relating to Goronwy Owen, and I'm informed that someone else was just in the other day researching the poet. (What?!) The nice librarian (Is there any other kind?) takes us to a back room of archival material and pulls out for me several folders labeled "Goronwy Owen." I settle down at a table with this material while the librarian locates for Randy the county's record books that might shed light on his own search.

There is no order to the papers I examine, and much of the information is already familiar to me. I conclude that most of the documents once belonged to the Rev. Edwin Williams, the erstwhile rector of St. Andrew's who led the effort to create the monument to Owen. I am interested to find what appears to be a general solicitation on "The Goronwy Owen Memorial Fund" letterhead. Dated December 1957, this letter is signed by Mr. Harry M. Meacham, President of the Poetry Society of Virginia, and the Fund co-chairmen, Professor John Hughes of McGill University in Montreal and the Rev. Maldwyn A. Davies of Washington, D. C. The letter begins:

> Why are the Welsh people on both sides of the Atlantic concerned about the Rev. Goronwy Owen, clergyman, poet, hymnologist, and teacher who has been dead 188 years? Why? Because he was the giant of the Welsh Bards and is still unsurpassed. Authorities rank his greatest work "The Last Day of Judgment" on a par with Milton's "Paradise Lost"; and his next best, "An Ode to Lewis Morris" written in St. Andrew's Parish, Brunswick County, Virginia, where he served the last nine years of his life and is buried, as one of the greatest literary feats in the Welsh language. And yet he was the poet whose intricate metres the postman, the farmer, and the policeman quoted.

The letter then explains that a tablet in Owen's honor was placed in Bangor Cathedral in Bangor, North Wales in 1831. Furthermore, in 1850, the Honourable Society of the Cymmrodorion wished to erect a monument at Owen's grave, but it could not be determined "where in Brunswick County he was buried." Just last year, the letter notes, a plaque to Owen was unveiled in the Library of the College of William and Mary during the Jamestown celebration.

> Now, "The Poetry Society of Virginia," recognizing the genius of Goronwy Owen, and knowing that proper recognition in St. Andrew's Parish, Brunswick County, Virginia, is long overdue, is sponsoring the project to perpetuate the memory Of Goronwy Owen by erecting a typically Welsh monument. This will be in the form of a Celtic cross, inscribed (in Welsh and in English) as follows:
>
> I Ogoneddu Duw Ac I Goffau
> Goronwy Owen (1723–1769)
> Clerigwr, Bardd, Gwladgarwr, Emynydd,
> Athro, Llythyrwr, Ysgolhaig Clasurol,
> Cymmrodor, A Saer-Rhydd
> Codwyd Y Gof-Adail Hon Gan Gymry Gogledd America
> A Chymdeithas Awen Virginia
> ***
> To The Glory Of God And In Memory Of
> Goronwy Owen (1723–1769)
> Clergyman, Poet, Patriot, Hymnologist,
> Teacher, Letter-Writer, Classical Scholar,
> Cymmrodor And Freemason.
> This Monument Was Erected By The Welsh People Of North America And The Poetry Society Of Virginia.

The letter continues:

> We are therefore writing to you, appealing to you as a lover of Wales and of things Welsh, or as one who values antiquities everywhere, for a contribution to help complete this task and thereby memorialize for all time this great cultural benefactor of the Welsh people.

As the letter goes on to explain, funds are needed by January 1 so that a contract for the monument may be placed in hopes that it will be ready by March 2. The letter notes that "since some contributions have come in," a large sum is not needed. "About $950 [total] will be sufficient" and the letter's recipient is asked to send a donation to the Rev. Edwin T. Williams.

There are multiple carbon copies of this letter in the files so the scope of the appeal must have been a broad one. Included in Mr. Williams' papers is an invitation to the unveiling, in the guise of another appeal, and this document itself is three typewritten pages. It begins,

Goronwy and Me

> Monument To Goronwy Owen
> To Be Unveiled
> On St. David's Sunday
> The Poetry Society of Virginia
> Requests the honor of your presence
> At the unveiling service of
> > The Goronwy Owen Memorial Monument
> > Saint David's Sunday March Second
> > Nineteen Hundred and Fifty-Eight
> > At half-past two o'clock
> > Saint Andrew's Protestant Episcopal Church
> > Saint Andrew's Parish
> > Brunswick County
> > Lawrenceville, Virginia
>
> This invitation is issued to all Welshmen throughout the United States and Canada and abroad as it will be their "day of glory." At last, after 188 years a suitable monument to Goronwy Owen, the giant of the Welsh Bards, still unsurpassed, will be placed in the Parish where he did his last work and is buried. The monument to be unveiled in St. Andrew's Churchyard in the quiet Southside Virginia town of Lawrenceville will be the gift of the Welsh people throughout the United States and Canada and the members of the Poetry Society of Virginia. The Association for the Preservation of Virginia Antiquities has also shown its interest in the project by being the first to make a sizeable contribution. And the Supreme Council of Scottish Rite Freemasonry has followed suit. Lawrenceville is seventy miles southwest of Richmond, Virginia.

The invitation goes on to state that there will be a memorial service in the church following the unveiling. There will also be an opportunity to go to the County Court House to see records pertaining to Owen as well as a six-mile pilgrimage to the traditional gravesite. There follows a litany of invited guests and the assertion "and from many other points Welshmen will be present to fill the air with praise." The invitation then provides a one-paragraph summary of the efforts to honor Owen in his land of exile. The invitation concludes with,

> The members of The Poetry Society of Virginia consider it a privilege to sponsor the monument to the long neglected clergyman, scholar and poet and have ordered the stone cut and arranged the unveiling ceremonies in the certain faith that the Welsh people of North America will do their share. As of this moment $550.00 is still needed. Have you sent your check yet to the treasurer? Please

Goronwy Celebrated

send it today to the Goronwy Owen Memorial Fund, c/o the Rev. Edwin T. Williams, Rector, St. Andrew's Episcopal Church, Lawrenceville, Virginia.

I find also a program for the events of March 2, 1958. It is eight half-pages, folded and stapled with a drawing on the front of the sanctuary of St. Andrew's, "The Mother Parish of Southside Virginia." Appended under the illustration is a brief history of the Parish which concludes that the present church "is believed to be the oldest public building now standing in Brunswick County." Page two lists the order of events for the memorial dedication which commences with "Welcome to Brunswick County and Lawrenceville" from the Hon. W. L. Heartwell, Jr." The monument is then unveiled by the Brunswick Masonic Lodge and "visiting Welsh Masons" and presented to "Saint Andrew's Parish, Brunswick County, and the Town of Lawrenceville" by Harry M. Meacham—on behalf of The Poetry Society of Virginia—and Professor John Hughes—on behalf of the Welsh People of the United States and Canada. The Hon. A. S. Harrison, Jr. (family friend and then Attorney General of Virginia) "receives" the monument and Arthur P. Gray, III and Elizabeth S. Gray offer comments on "The Rev. Arthur P. Gray, Jr., David Lloyd, and Goronwy Owen." There is a prayer of dedication by The Right Rev. George P. Gunn, Bishop of the Diocese of Southern Virginia and the singing (in Welsh and English) of "Land of my Fathers," Hymn No. 76 in the Gymanfa Ganu Hymnal.

Page three of the program features the inscriptions found on the monument, already referred to in the "letter of invitation." Page four details the order of the memorial service, "Following partially, The Order for Evening Prayer, Daily throughout the Year, from the Prayer Book of the Church of England used in St. Andrew's Parish by the Rev. Goronwy Owen." I'm interested to note that the sermon, by Professor John Hughes, is apparently on the "'Ode to Lewis Morris' written by Goronwy Owen in Brunswick County July 20, 1767 and considered his "second best." A portion of the poem is read in Welsh and English by the Rev. Maldwyn Davies. The offertory anthem is Owen's own—and only—hymn in Welsh, found on page seven of the program and translated by John Hughes. The music for the service is provided by members of The Saint David's Welsh American Society of Washington, D. C. with Mrs. G. R. Thomas accompanying. A note at the bottom of page four reads, "Refreshments will be served in the Parish House immediately following the Service." Of course, this is why my mother doesn't remember the service itself; she was in the Parish House kitchen preparing food for the reception!

Page five lists the particulars for the visits to the County Clerk's Office and the Pilgrimage to the Traditional Grave Site of the Rev. Goronwy Owen. Also included on page five is a translation by Maldwyn Davies of "Elegy to Lewis Morris" (first stanza of 189 lines) as well as a few "notes on Goronwy Owen." Page six provides a list of "Participants and Distinguished Guests," while page eight, the back of the program, catalogues the 1958 church directory of lay leaders. All in all, it must have been a grand event, and I'm sorry I never asked Daddy about it when I had the chance.

Randy and I leave the library and on our way back to my van, I stop into the office of the *Brunswick Times Gazette*, Lawrenceville's weekly newspaper. I'm interested to see if there might be any newspaper articles regarding the dedication. The lady at the front desk points me to the big books of back issues and I locate the book for 1958. In the issue published February 27th (Volume 70, No. 9), I find a front-page article with the headline, "Monument to the Late Goronwy Owen, Poet and Rector, to Be Unveiled Here." In seven short paragraphs, this piece gives the particulars of the planned ceremony, which of course is familiar to me now. Other front-page items include an announcement of the "Miss Brunswick High School 1958" contest to be held the following night, February 28. A column on the left side of the page is headed "Brunswick Stew" and I take it that this is a regular feature of random musings. This week's installment is about the Southern expression "you all" and reprints a poem from the Christian Science Monitor which begins,

> "Come all of you from other parts
> Both city folks and rural,
> And listen while I tell you this:
> The word 'you-all' is plural."

I search subsequent issues for any mention of the ceremony itself, but find nothing. With the office lady's kind permission, I wrestle the 1958 book onto the copier, and after repeated tries manage to reproduce the appropriate section of the front page.

It is hot now, and Randy and I decide to start our trek homeward. First, however, we will detour by Dolphin in search of Goronwy's grave. With Randy navigating, we wind our way over the unlined pavement the six miles or so to the post office in this tiny Brunswick County hamlet. We walk into the low-slung cinderblock building and I introduce myself to the woman behind the counter, who, upon hearing my name asks if I'm related to Alison Heartwell. Apparently, the postmistress had attended high school with my sister. Pleasantries aside, I express my interest in visiting the gravesite of Owen and she, Betty Wynn, suggests I talk to Wayne Gilley. She knows Wayne is at home; she calls him, and Randy and I walk next door to meet him in the front yard of his home. Again, I introduce myself and Wayne immediately asks, "Are you Sonny Heartwell's boy?" I reply in the affirmative, and Wayne says he is happy to take us to the gravesite and what remains of Owen's house. We climb into the cab of Wayne's truck (my van deemed unsuitable for the trek), and drive a mile or two on the paved road before Wayne abruptly darts into an opening along the road's edge. There is a dirt path of sorts that he follows and he carefully maneuvers his Ford through rutted and rocky ditches. At one point, Randy gets out to pull back a sapling obstructing our way, and after about a mile, the "road" peters out and we get out of the truck.

    A short walk through weeds and scrub pines brings us to the house, a decayed, listing shell of a structure. According to Gay Neale's book, the Owen house had "a foundation of uncoursed fieldstone laid randomly" and was a prime example of "a simple design with one or two rooms over a cellar, with a jump, a tiny dormered room overhead reached by a narrow winding stair."[7] Definitely not a grand plantation home, I think, as I bushwhack around its perimeter snapping pictures. Wayne then leads us to the marker at the gravesite, which he believes was located by Earl Williams, managing partner of the local funeral home founded by my grandfather. According to Wayne, Mr. Williams researched how the Welsh buried their dead and learned that traditionally four stones were stuck in the ground at the corners of the grave. Mr. Williams found such an arrangement and deemed the spot best for the placement of the marker installed in time for the monument dedication ceremony. The marker reads, "The Traditional Grave Site of The Rev. Goronwy Owen, 1723–1769" and rests in the shade of two venerable cedars. I take pictures of this stone that's dappled with shadows, and we make our way back to Wayne's truck. I hop in the back, content to let the breeze cool me off during the ten-minute drive, and I'm happy to have walked the same ground trod by Owen over 240 years ago.

    Wayne invites us in when we arrive back at his house, but we decline, eager to hit the road. I offer to give Wayne "a little something for his time," but he'll have nothing of it. Randy and I thank him, and in my van we

---

7. Neale, *Brunswick County*, 106–7.

meander our way back to the interstate. On the way home, we detour through Louisa County, to look for Long Creek, located near the community of Apple Grove; this is Randy's "ancestral home." We do find the creek and we snap a few obligatory photos of it.

It's about 7:00 p.m. when I drop Randy off at his house. It's been a full, rich day that leaves me marveling at the many intersections of past and present. As I head home to Susie and dinner, I conclude that Goronwy Owen was likely a difficult man to befriend, but I am nonetheless happy to have further made his acquaintance.

PART II

Goronwy'R Alltud
(Goronwy the Exile)

6

July, 1761

**FROM CYWYDD Y MAEN GWERTHFAWR
(PRECIOUS STONE)
by Goronwy Owen**

> I have been searching for that which is above worldly riches
> And, after searching, made my return;
> Searching for a gem of fine, pure aspect
> More pure than the jasper stone.
> It was a remarkable fair gem,
> Brilliant in its appearance, and it was Contentment.

Goronwy and Me

A CLOUD OF MOSQUITOES droned about Goronwy Owen's dark-complexioned face. As he stood on the banks of Reedy Creek, he slapped at the insects in the oppressive Virginia heat and recalled again the cool sea breezes of his native Anglesey. There was no use dwelling on the past, he knew, yet he longed for Môn and the sound of the language he loved. In his three years in this colony, he had met only one or two other Welshmen, and certainly there were none to be found here in the frontier of Brunswick. Even his son, Robert, the only surviving child of his first marriage, ignored the Cymric tongue of his ancestors. Just as well, perhaps; a new land requires a new language. Pulling down his hat, Owen set off again to complete his survey.

He had already walked this parcel with William Cocke, its owner. Cocke, of Lunenburg County, was willing to sell the 400 acres for £90, a sum Owen found staggering. In England, he had never earned more than £50, but his salary here gave him hope. However, he knew that like most clergymen he would need to supplement his income. He could start a school—God knows the local population was an illiterate one—but he had been frustrated leading recalcitrant learners in the grammar schools of Pwllheli and Denbigh. And certainly there would be no Greek and Latin scholars here like his former pupils at the college in Williamsburg, students such as young red-headed Thomas Jefferson, who had such an aptitude for classical languages and who played violin at the lavish parties thrown by Governor Fauquier.

He could farm. Tobacco and cotton bloomed as far as the eye could see and black slaves could be bought at market, like any other commodity. The Greeks and Romans had enslaved whole populations, and, through "the curse of Ham," his King James Bible sanctioned the practice. Yes, he could farm, raise a family again. He was only thirty-seven years old, and soon Robert would be an adult, eager to forge his own path.

How far the poet had traveled. Only five years previous, Owen was settled as a curate in Northolt under Dr. Samuel Nicholls. Owen had been disappointed that the scheme, fostered by the Morris brothers, for a Welsh chaplaincy in London, had not been realized. Plagued by discontent and want, Owen again had resorted to drink, and, on September 6, 1756, Lewis wrote to William that Goronwy stood to lose his position because of drunkenness and debt. The next month a distress warrant was executed on the poet's furniture and the Vicar was soon forced to withhold Owen's salary to pay his mounting debts. Also, Owen was accused of spending the surplice money on his own personal needs.

The Morris brothers were put out with Owen. William remained upset by Owen's failure to return *The Leather Harp*, a borrowed rare manuscript, and Lewis was preoccupied with his mining interest in Wales. His once ardent desire to publish Owen's poems had cooled; he did not want to see the poet literally drink the profits that might accrue from publication. It was at this point that Dr. Nicholls intervened by appealing to his friend Thomas Sherlock, Bishop of London. Sherlock was formerly Bishop of Bangor and was known to be generous to his Welsh curates, and Nicholls was the Bishop's private chaplain and confidant. As Bishop of London, Sherlock served as Chancellor of the College of William and Mary, and when a vacancy on the faculty emerged, Nicholls recommended Owen to Sherlock. The position was offered to Owen, and when Goronwy accepted, Nicholls even tendered him the service of his personal cook to assist him in establishing a dignified home in Williamsburg.

The vacancy in Williamsburg had arisen because its previous incumbent, the Rev. Thomas Robinson, was "incapable of discharging the duties of his office as Master of the Grammar School." The Board of Visitors appealed to the Bishop to not appoint another clergyman as the demands of ministering often resulted in the neglect of the school and its students. "Therefore," the Visitors beseeched, "his Lordship will be pleased that the person to be sent over be a Layman, if such a one may be procured; but if not, a clergyman." Ironically, the Visitors' complaint with Robinson involved his "Immoral conduct, being often drunk and [a] very bad example to the students."[1] Welcome, Goronwy Owen!

Owen arrived in Williamsburg in March, 1758 after his horrific three-month voyage from London. Having lost his wife and youngest son at sea, Owen's troubles were far from over. Thomas Robinson refused to surrender his keys to the Grammar Master's apartment, and "the President ordered Hasps with Staples and Paddlocks to be put upon the Doors of the several apartments and Schools and two new Locks upon the Wicket doors."[2]

Owen began his duties on April 5th and two days later he took an oath of allegiance in which he acknowledged, "That the King's Majesty under God is the only Supreme Governor of this Realm." He also "subscribed" to the 39 Articles of Religion from 1562, and reaffirmed, "That the Book of

---

1. Thomas, "William and Mary," 29.
2. Ibid., 31.

Common Prayer and of ordering Bishops, Priests, and Deacons containeth nothing in it contrary to the Word of God."[3]

The College of William and Mary was sixty-five years old when Owen first set foot on its grounds, and the school was organized into three departments: the College proper, which contained a Philosophy and Divinity School; the Grammar School; and the Indian School. Though appointed Master of the Grammar School, Owen was also deemed a Professor of Humanity and undoubtedly taught in the College as well. The Grammar School was characterized as follows:

> To the school belongs a schoolmaster and if the number of scholars require it an usher. The Schoolmaster is one of the six masters of whom with the President and scholars the College consists . . . Let there be paid a yearly salary to the schoolmaster 80 pounds sterling 2 and 20 shillings from each scholar by the year when there is no usher. But if there be an usher too in that school let 15 shillings be paid to the master and 5 shillings to the usher and for a yearly salary let there be paid to the usher 50 pounds sterling. But from the poor scholars who are upon any charitable foundation neither the master nor usher are to ask any school wages but are to be taught gratis.[4]

The "philosophy" of the Grammar School is further delineated, thusly: "In the Grammar School let the Latin and Greek tongues be well taught, we assign 4 yrs to the Latin and 2 to the Greek. As for Rudiments and Grammars and Classick authors of each Tongue let them teach the same books which by law or custom are used in the Schools of England."[5]

Additionally, "Special care likewise must be taken of their morals that none of the scholars presume to tell a lie or curse or swear or to take or do anything obscene or quarrel and fight or play at cards or dice or set in to drinking or do anything else that is contrary to good manners." Finally, "The Master shall likewise take care that all the scholars learn the Church of England Catechism in the Vulgar tongue and that they who are further advanced learn it likewise in Latin."[6]

---

3. Ibid.
4. Thomas, "William and Mary," 25–26.
5. Ibid., 26.
6. Ibid.

It is clear, then, that Owen confronted high expectations when he assumed his position. The code of behavior for the students was no less detailed:

> Ordered 1st that no Boy shall be permitted to saunter away his time upon any of the college steps, or to be seen during School Hours, under a severe admonishment [?] from the President or any of the Masters.
> Ordered 2nd that no boy presume to go into the Kitchen or cause any Disturbance there under a severe punishment from the President or any of the Masters.
> Ordered 3rd that the Boys regularly attend Dinner and Supper in the Hall, and the Housekeeper be strictly charged and commended not to allow any victuals whatever to be sent into Private Rooms to any Boys excepting to such as are really sick.[7]

The political climate of Williamsburg was surely bubbling with uncertainty as fractious relations with the Mother Country were starting to foment. George Washington and George Mason were members of the House of Burgesses in 1759. The next year they would be joined by Patrick Henry, who in 1762, made a name for himself in the "Parsons' Cause," a case to determine whether the price of tobacco should be set by the colonial government or the Crown.

Owen paused in the shade of two white oaks and mopped his brow. He knelt on the creek's red-clay bank, and cupping his hands, carefully scooped water from the slow-moving stream. The water was tepid at best and did little to quench his thirst. He gazed through the limp leaves overhead to gauge the position of the sun and judged the time to be close to noon. He had stayed last night at the ordinary on the Plank Road, its prices conspicuously posted inside the front door:

The following rates of Liquor are set for the year: "Rum by the gallon, ten shillings. Brandy by the gallon, Twenty shillings. English Cyder by the Quart, one shilling, sixpence. Virginia Cyder, by the Quart, sixpence. For a breakfast, sevenpence, half penny. Lodging for one night with good bed, covering of clean sheets, sixpence; pasturage one day and night, sixpence."[8]

The night had been a restless one of drink and card-playing, and the barbaric spectacle of the cock fight lingered in his memory.

---

7. Ibid., 28.
8. Neale, *Brunswick County*, 51.

Goronwy and Me

Today, he had left his lodgings early, after his morning prayer at dawn, and walked the four miles to this site. He was a vigorous hiker, even in such stifling humidity, but his clothes were wet with perspiration from exertion and last night's rum. He pulled a piece of dried beef from his rucksack and proceeded to eat it slowly, meditatively. He thought again of Williamsburg and his life there. He knew God to be merciful, and it was not his place to question His plan. But yet... but yet...

Sometime between August and October, 1958—just a few months after his appointment in Williamsburg—Owen married Mrs. Clayton, the widowed sister of Thomas Dawson, president of the College. But, as is reported in the minutes of the staff meeting on August 28, 1759, "Mrs. Martha Bryan appointed Housekeeper of the College in place of Mrs. Owen deceased."[9] Owen had now lost two wives in less than two years.

Owen attended the monthly staff meetings of the College during the first half of 1760. The notes of these sessions cite no misbehavior on Owen's part. However, the minutes of the meetings of the College Visitors and Governors tell another story. On April 26th, the record alleges, "That Mr. Rowe, one of the Professors of Philosophy, and Mr. Owen, Professor of Humanity, have been often seen scandalously drunk in College and in the public streets of Williamsburg and York. That the said Mr. Rowe and Mr. Owen frequently utter horrid oaths and execrations in their common conversation... Mr. Rowe is undermining the discipline of the President of the College and Mr. Owen has been guilty of the same behaviour."[10]

Owen is not mentioned again in the official records, although on April 30th Jacob Rowe is summoned before the Board and pleads guilty to all charges, excepting insubordination. In a subsequent meeting, Rowe vows to reform his behavior. It is likely that Owen managed to avoid disapprobation because of the influence of his brother-in-law, President Dawson.

Mr. Rowe's reformation was short-lived. On August 14th, it was reported that he, "did lately lead the boys against the Town Apprentices to a Pitched Battle with Pistols and other Weapons instead of restraining and keeping them in as was the duty of his office to have done,"[11] and he was dismissed from his position. Although Owen is not mentioned in this dispatch, it is clear that he collaborated in this fight with his friend, the

9. Thomas, "William and Mary," 32.
10. Ibid., 34.
11. Ibid.

Professor of Moral Philosophy. One account has him wielding a bull-whip during the fray. The genesis of this altercation is explained by Hywel M. Davies, as follows:

> It was the custom in Williamsburg on a Sunday for the students to be seated as a body in the gallery of Bruton parish church where the President of the College, Thomas Dawson was minister. The townspeople sat below. According to 'Tim Pastime'[a satirical essay of the era related to the Parsons' Cause], the collegians mistook the upward-turned gaze of the townsmen as a form of mockery and 'in return for the unopposed insult collected all the saliva they could and steamed it on the Oppidans faces, nay some have asserted that the urinary conduits were exercised on the occasion.' After Church, the townsmen threatened 'universal carnage, if such indignities were repeated.' Goronwy Owen and Jacob Rowe took up the challenge and announced 'War against the Townsmen' to redeem their 'seminary' from its peril.[12]

The minutes of the Journal of the President and the Masters for September 25th note, "The Revd. Mr. William Webb (at a meeting of the Visitors and Governors held the 14th August, 1760) having been elected Master of the Grammar School in the place of the Revd. Goronwy Owen who resigned did this day enter upon his said office."[13] It is apparent Owen quit his post to escape dismissal.

Over twenty years later in England, a former acquaintance of the poet's sought to learn what had befallen Owen in Virginia. This friend, the Rev. Edward Owen, made many queries after the displaced Welshman. Finally, in 1795, Edward Owen received news that shed light on Goronwy's experience in Williamsburg. In a letter to the Rev. Mr. Williams of Llanrwst, Edward Owen writes:

> Warrington, October 27, 1795.
>
> Dear Sir,—It was not till this day that I received any authentic account concerning Goronwy Owen. It comes from Mr. Thomas Davies, a Virginia clergyman, the son of a Liverpool gentleman, who, failing in business at home about the year 1754, contrived to get into Orders, and went with his family to Virginia, and got a Living, which his son, I believe, possesses now as his successor. The intelligence, therefore, which I have been long soliciting, without success, from some of the Liverpool merchants, is come at last

12. Davies, "Parsons' Cause," 55.
13. Thomas, "William and Mary," 35.

Goronwy and Me

through this channel to a clergyman in Liverpool, an old scholar of mine, Mr. Blundell, Chaplain of St. Georges's.

Mr. Davies's letter is as follows:

Virginia, Alexandria, August 1st, 1795.

Your favour of the 20th December last mistook its way strangely, as it came to my hand only a few days ago. I thank you, my dear sir, for the civilities it contains; and proceed to give you the information which your friend is anxious to receive.

In November 1758, the time I was sent to the Grammar School in the College of William and Mary in Williamsburg, the Rev. Gronovius Owen was a master of that school. He was a blunt, hasty-tempered Welshman, and esteemed a good Latin and Greek scholar. He married a Mrs. Clayton, who at that time was Dame of the College. She shortly died without issue. He had two sons, Robert and Gronovius, who came from England with him. I remember him well, as he was frequently at my father's, and very fond of talking Welsh with my mother.

Rum, which has destroyed more than the sword, was his destruction. He was extremely intemperate; and in one of his merry frolics he and a Mr. Rowe, who was Professor of Moral Philosophy, headed the Collegians in a fray which they had with the young men of the town; for which and other flagrant improprieties they were dismissed from their offices by the Visitors.

This, I think, happened in the year 1760. Mr. Rowe returned to England, and Mr. Owen was soon after inducted into a parish in Brunswick County, Virginia. The son Gronovius died in a short time; Mr. Owen lived only a few years; and soon after it was reported that Robert also was dead. I fancy this account may be relied on, as I never heard of Robert afterwards.

Mr. Blundell, who is now here, tells me that Mr. Sporling, who is a merchant in Liverpool, has written also to some friend of his upon the same subject. I think you wished to enquire whether Goronwy left any papers behind him. It is a thing hardly to be expected; but as Mr. Sporling may probably seek his intelligence through some other channel, perhaps something more may arise.

I shall be very happy to hear of your welfare, and
I am, dear Sir,
Your respectful and faithful, humble Servant,
E. Owen[14]

---

14. Jones, *Poetical Works (Vol. II)*, 286–88.

July, 1761

Owen finished his repast. He followed again the meanders of the creek to a sloping pine before turning southwest through a field to climb a small promontory bordered by a grove of cedars. Here he would build his house, facing east towards Môn, and a small barn could be situated nearby. The acres between this site and the stream would be suitable to pasture a few horses and cows. There seemed to be ample fieldstone for a foundation and the tall, straight oaks behind him would provide lumber for framing a modest, unpretentious dwelling. The land was rich, no question, and convenient to the two chapels of the parish. Yes, it would do nicely. Here, God willing, he and a wife could raise children upon whom he could shower affection.

He must prove the Vestry wrong. They had not wanted him; that much was clear. But they and the people of the parish, Llan Andreas, would grow to respect him, respect his learning, his erudition. Again, he vowed to abstain from drink, and now, on this hilltop, he asked God to cleanse him from sin as he recited the healing words of the General Confession:

> ALMIGHTY and most merciful Father; We have erred, and strayed from thy ways like lost sheep. We have followed too much the devices and desires of our own hearts. We have offended against thy holy laws. We have left undone those things which we ought to have done; And we have done those things which we ought not to have done; And there is no health in us. But thou, O Lord, have mercy upon us, miserable offenders. Spare thou them, O God, who confess their faults. Restore thou them that are penitent; According to thy promises declared unto mankind in Christ Jesus our Lord. And grant, O most merciful Father, for his sake; That we may hereafter live a godly, righteous, and sober life, To the glory of thy holy Name. Amen.

As the crow flies, Brunswick County is about 75 miles from Williamsburg, and Owen arrived there just 10 days after his resignation from the College of William and Mary. He had with him a letter of recommendation to the Vestry of St. Andrew's Parish from Francis Fauquier, "His Majestic Lieutenant Governor and Commander in Chief of the Colony and Dominion of Virginia." Owen's arrival in Brunswick created a serious dilemma for the Vestry which had already promised to hand over the reins of the parish to the Rev. Patrick Lunnan. The benefice had been vacant for a few months since the death in the spring of the Rev. George Purdie. The parish had been unhappy under the leadership of the Rev. Purdie. He was "intemperate" and had even been presented to the Bishop's commissary for trial before a pledge of reform and good behavior.

In general, during this era, the clergy who emigrated from England were of mediocre ability. The parish priests often lived isolated existences with few books or cultural diversions. Housing was often inadequate and the salary subject to the whimsical prices of the tobacco crop. In most parishes there was a flat salary rate of 16,000 pounds per year, plus another 1,200 pounds "for cask and shrinkage." There might be some "glebe land" on which a minister could further plant, and some clergymen acquired additional property and became active growers. But as the price of tobacco fluctuated, so did a priest's salary, a situation that led to the aforementioned "Parsons' Cause." In 1752, the House of Burgesses had passed the "Two Penny Act" which stipulated that no minister could receive the excess value of tobacco if the price rose above two pence per pound. Clergy also supplemented their income with fees for weddings, funerals, baptisms, and Easter offerings, all which could enhance a minister's income by fifty percent.

Faced with Owen's sudden arrival at St. Andrew's, the Vestry resolved, "that the Reverend Gentlemen Mr. Patrick Lunan and Mr. Gronow Owen be received into this Parish as Probationers untill the tenth day of November next and that they be paid the usual salary for a Minister to be divided between them in proportion to the time of their attendance in the said Parish." However, cognizant of its obligation to colonial authority, the Vestry further acknowledged that, "your Honour [Fauquier] may in the mean Time make Presentation into the Parish of such Minister as your Honour shall please." But, as the Vestry concluded, "We therefore humbly petition your Honour that in your Clemency you'll suffer us to make trial of those Gentlemen and at the expiration of such Time choose for ourselves."[15]

Despite the Vestry's plea, on September 10th the Governor granted a "presentation, instituting, collating, and inducting the Reverend Gronow Owen into the Parish of St. Andrew's." Yet, Vestry records from December make clear that Owen was not welcomed with open arms. "The Vestry having made a trial of the Reverend Mr. Patrick Lunan and the Reverend Mr. Gronow Owen according to an order of Vestry dated 25th day of August 1760 do make choice of neither of the said gentlemen as minister of this Parish."[16] Still, at this same December meeting, the Vestry paid off Lunan who before the end of the year was Rector of Suffolk Church. There he endured a contentious relationship with his parish until his resignation in 1775, having managed to actually avoid preaching for many years.

15. Thomas, "Rector of St. Andrew's," 118.
16. Ibid., 119.

July, 1761

Owen, therefore, embarked on an interim period until the Governor's mandate became legal on June 22, 1761. The Governor's letter was accepted as official at a Vestry meeting on that day. Also, "It was further ordered that the Revd. Mr. Gronow Owen's salary begins on New year's Day last" and "that the Collector pay unto the Reverend Mr. Gronow Owen for six months salary 8500 lbs Tobacco.[17]" Owen became one of the signatories of Vestry meeting minutes from this day forward.

Full of resolve, Owen left the shade of the cedar grove, and following a deer path through the woods, made his way back to the road. The sun was high now, and the walk back to the ordinary would be a hot one. He would spend the night there before returning to the temporary rectory in the morning. This very night, he would write to William Cocke to make arrangements for purchasing the property. He would speak to John Lightfoot, and seek his advice. Lightfoot would know who to hire to build his house and to clear land for next year's tobacco crop.

There was much to be done, he knew. But through judicious thought and habit, he could do it. God in His wisdom had sent him here to live among apostates and heathens. But God would equip him to do the work of His kingdom, and though he was not deserving of it, the Lord would let His grace shine upon him.

"Lord, have mercy on me, for I am a sinner," Owen intoned as he set foot on the path to shelter, the path to refreshment, the path to renewal, the path to salvation.

---

17. Ibid., 119–20.

7

November, 1763

FROM CYWYDD Y GWAHODD
(THE INVITATION)
by Goronwy Owen
(Sent from Northolt, in the year 1755 to William Parry,
Deputy Comptroller of the Mint)

    Parry, of all my friends the best,
    Thou who thy maker cherishest,
    Thou who regard'st me so sincere,
    And who to me art no less dear;
    Kind friend, in London since thou art,
    To love thee's not my wisest part;
    This separation's hard to bear:
    To love thee not far better were.
    But wilt thou not from London town
    Journey some day to Northolt down,
    Song to obtain, O sweet reward,
    And walk the garden of the Bard?

    The rose, at edge of winter now,

November, 1763

Doth fade with all its summer glow;
Old are become the roses all,
Decline to age we also shall;
And with this prayer I'll end my lay,
Amen, with me, O Parry say;
To us be rest from all annoy,
And a robust old age of joy;
May we, ere pangs of death we know,
Back to our native Mona go;
May pleasant days us there await,
United and inseparate!
And the dread hour, when God shall please
To bid our mutual journey cease,
May Christ, who reigns in heaven above,
Receive us to his breast of love!

Goronwy and Me

"If we say that we have no sin, we deceive ourselves, and the truth is not in us; but if we confess our sins, God is faithful and just to forgive us our sins, and to cleanse us from all unrighteousness." As instructed by the 1662 Book of Common Prayer, the Rev. Goronwy Owen pronounced the familiar scripture "with a loud voice," a voice that despite its English utterances, still retained the phrasings and sensibilities of his native Welsh. He gazed upon the small congregation seated in the unheated church. It was his second service of the day, a day which had begun early at Kittlestick Chapel, named, he had learned, after a long paddle-like stick used in stirring the contents of a kettle when pork fat is being rendered into lard. He knew not the history of the connection between this paddle and a house of God, but considered it an apt metaphor for transforming the calumnious souls of his communicants. He would stir and stir, God's word the paddle, and render their souls into something serviceable.

After this service in the larger chapel of the parish, he would dine at the home of Thomas Simmons, his father-in-law. The meal would be ample, he knew. Last month's first frost had ushered in a season of butchering, and the salty ham he was so fond of would satisfy his growing hunger. Martha would likely serve from her larder the stewed tomatoes he found so enticing and so alien to his native fare. Yes, and the cobbler—apples wrapped in a warm crust, doused with thick cream. It was indeed a remarkable land, abundant with fish, fowl, game, and domesticated foodstuffs. Thank you Lord for your munificence!

The Simmons family was a respected one, and Owen considered himself fortunate to have won the heart of Joan, the youngest daughter. She was modest and deferential, and her dowry had nicely furnished his new house. She was young, scarcely older than Robert, and Owen had been delighted when just the week before she shyly informed him that she was with child. He prayed that God would bless him with a son, two of whom the Lord in his wisdom had already called home. He did not know how he could ever love another daughter. The memory of Elin, his angel, still haunted him. He could still see her dark curls framing her beatific face, could hear the cascading melody of her giggles and the sound of her slippered feet running across the floor in Walton as she leapt into his arms. Yes, sons were needed here in this place to work the land and manage the unfortunate negroes condemned to servitude.

Thomas and Martha would be happy to receive his news, he was certain. They had seen the wisdom of his suit, though they had not initially

November, 1763

embraced it, or him. They were not superstitious people, but the fact that he was twice-widowed gave them pause. Yet his plantation recommended him, and the parish was growing and there were souls to be saved. He was an educated man and ambitious. No, Joan could do much worse.

The congregation gazed expectantly at their bearded pastor. Kneeling, he led them through the General Confession, noting the cold breaths emanating from their mouths. Light streamed through the windows now as he, rising and lifting his right hand pronounced the Absolution: "He pardoneth and absolveth all them that truly repent, and unfeignedly believe his holy Gospel. Wherefore, let us beseech him to grant us true repentance, and his Holy Spirit, that those things may please him, which we do at this present; and that the rest of life hereafter may be pure, and holy; so that at last we may come to his eternal joy; through Jesus Christ our Lord."

"Amen," answered the penitents.

St. Andrew's Parish was established in 1732, and the members of its first vestry were each paid one thousand pounds of tobacco for their service. The first priest of the parish was the Rev. John Betty, and several churches were constructed during his tenure. The Vestry Book of the era describes these structures: "Forty foot long and twenty foot wide, each chapel to be shingled and weatherboarded with plank, two windows each side of each chapel same size of the windows in the church already built, one window at each end of both Chapels, Chancill windows same size of side windows. Two closed pews in each chapel; pulpit, gallory and four foot alley [aisle] each."[1]

Initially, the boundaries of St. Andrew's Parish were identical with those of Brunswick County. However, poor roads and swelling streams often made it difficult for all people of the parish to regularly attend worship services. Therefore, in 1754, the Virginia Assembly decreed that the portion of the county south of the Meherrin River would become its own distinct parish.

Everyone in the parish was deemed a member of the Established Church, which was supported by English law. The vestry of the parish was required to tithe its people, and each household was forced to contribute a bushel of corn and ten pounds of tobacco per year. In St. Andrew's, each tithable was also required to support the poor by paying one shilling, six pence each year. Additionally, a taxpayer was often obligated to pay a pound of tobacco if absent from church on a given Sunday or fifty pounds if absent

---

1. Neale, *Brunswick Coumty,"* 85.

for a month. Tobacco, of course, was also used to pay the minister, finance the building and maintaining of churches, and to provide for the poor and sick. The vestry was a powerful entity. Between 1758 and 1769, four of the six representatives from Brunswick County in the House of Burgesses were vestrymen of the parish: William Thornton, Edward Goodrich, Frederick Maclin, and Thomas Stith. The sheriffs of the county for this era were also members of the vestry.

The Rev. George Purdie succeeded the Rev. Betty as rector of St. Andrew's, and in 1757, he was reprimanded by the Vestry for some unknown transgression, but allowed to continue on the promise of good behavior. However, after his death in 1760, the parish begrudgingly welcomed its two "probationers," the Rev. Patrick Lunan and the Rev. Goronwy Owen.

The Rev. Goronwy Owen read The Collect for the First Sunday of Advent: "Almighty God, give us grace that we may cast away the works of darkness, and put upon us the armor of light, now in the time of this mortal life in which thy son Jesus Christ came to visit us in great humility; that in the last day, when he shall come again in his glorious majesty to judge both the quick and the dead, we may rise to the life immortal; through him who liveth and reigneth with thee and the Holy Ghost, one God, now and forever. Amen."

Did they know, did they understand, the gravity of these words? Would they, could they "cast away the works of darkness"? Silently, Owen prayed that this band of sinners, with himself at its head, would don the "armor of light" and follow Jesus' example. The stakes were high and irreversible. He must be an example to his parishioners, he must live a "godly, righteous, and sober life." Joan, blessed Iona, would help him. He had not had a drink of rum in the six months of their marriage. And why should he? He had no need for false intoxicants as he and Joan forged their life together. Their home was trim and neat, an example of propriety thanks to her efforts and those of Peg Old, their negro house servant. Joan understood and appreciated the rhythms of his calling, his need for quiet prayer and reflection, and the taxing demands of ministering to the sick and dying. Often, he would return home late, having again administered last rites in some remote corner of the parish. On the way, he would pass an ordinary and its allure of strong drink. But he would not, must not, pause; he knew Joan's warm embrace and eager body would provide refreshment enough.

November, 1763

And the plantation showed promise. The first harvests of tobacco and cotton had gained a profit, thanks to Robert's careful attention and the faithful labors of the do boys, Bob and Stephen. Owen had no heart for physical labor, unaccustomed as he was to it, but Robert thrived working in the fields, overseeing every detail of the farm's execution. Yet, Robert would not always be there, Owen knew. He would marry and establish his own life as ordained in the scriptures.

Yes, Owen must strive to live, like Christ, in "great humility." He would fail, of course, but this life was a constant battle and the enemy, Satan, never rested. However, on the day of judgment, Owen prayed he would "rise to the life immortal."

"Cywydd Y Farn Fawr" ("The Day of Judgment") is considered Owen's finest and best-known poem. Written during his curacy in Donnington, Owen refers to this effort in his letters more than any other work. Apparently, it significantly occupied his time and attention, and he was proud of its execution. As was Lewis Morris. In his "introduction" to the poem, Morris writes, "I shall venture my own reputation thus far, in giving the poem before us its due character, at least as far as my knowledge in these things goes from about forty years' study and experience: that it doth not, in my opinion, come short of anything I have hitherto met in our language."[2]

Morris continues, "The subject is the grandest in the world, being an account or description of that awful, great tribunal, the Last Day of Judgment; a subject which every true Christian believes and expects."[3]

The poem is clearly inspired by the Book of Revelations. As Owen's biographer, the Rev. Robert Jones, writes:

> The poet's recital of the stirring events of the great Day of Judgment is founded almost entirely on the Sacred Volume. He not only tells us this, but asseverates it again and again, to leave no doubt as to the source whence he derived his information. The term 'Word,' as applied to the Holy Scriptures, is mentioned four or five times within the compass of as many lines; but with such artistic ability, that it in no way offends by its redundancy either of thought or expression. Whatever may have been the defects of the last century in doctrine or life, there were none of that caviling at

---

2. Jones, *Poetical Works (Vol. I)*, 22.
3. Ibid.

the Bible, or denial of its plenary inspiration, which is so prominently the feature of the nineteenth century.[4]

According to Branwen Jarvis, 'Judgment' "lacks dramatic impact" in "its beginning and end." Still, "some of the middle passages are masterly." As Jarvis asserts:

> Goronwy describes the earth in tumult on the Day of Judgement in lines which bend cynghannedd magnificently to his own will. The correspondence of sense and sound is stunning:
>
> The hideous furnace mouths of the entire pit of hell
> Fall through the depths into the abyss;
> The impassable wall will lie in ruins
> Henceforth, all bulging and crooked;
> The hellish family of demons tremble
> And the devil himself trembles and takes fright;
> The Evil One seeks his cauldron,
> He loves to lurk in the depths of darkness.
>
> The effect of such passages is enhanced by Goronwy's confident and inventive use of compounds, and also by his carefully contrasting use of passages which have quieter and smoother rhythms and sound-patterns.[5]

All three of the Morris brothers were effusive in their praise of this poem. In May of 1752, William wrote Richard to say that acting on Goronwy's behalf, he would ask a Mr. Ellis to print "Cywydd y Farn." Apparently, Mr. Ellis declined the request, or at least had reservations regarding the poem, which seems to have prompted a petulant reply from Owen. In a letter to William Morris, Goronwy writes:

> I am sorry my letter to Mr. Ellis was not kind enough. I think I thanked him for that and all other favours. What! Did he expect that I should burst out into ecstasies and launch forth into a panegyric on his extraordinary erudition and deep skill in his mother's tongue—a specimen whereof he had sent enclosed in his letter? I was not so well bred as to learn to flatter; and if that was not what he expected, I am not sorry that he was disappointed. I thought the doctor had been a man of sound ears, and could take up with truth in its own native dress, without the bawd's tricks and whorish garb of soothing and flattery. I have known him of old

---

4. Ibid., 25.
5. Jarvis, *Goronwy Owen*. 64–65.

to be of a morose, peevish temper; an instance whereof he gave me when in your house at Holyhead; for having given me a thesis to make a theme on, when I waited on him with it, made I suppose in the best manner I was then able, and which was in no way contemptible, considering my years, the good Doctor, expecting, I conceive, I should have outdone himself and Tom Brown too, fell into such extravagancy of passion as little became him, crying, "What stuff is here! Out upon it! I have done with you! I don't want your Latin, I can make good Latin myself (a wonder for a Fellow of the College)," and a great deal more to the same purpose. Now I might as well have sent him back his Welsh paper with a "What stuff! I can write better Welsh myself"—a greater wonder—"and I don't want it," &c., &c. And I might have added likewise, "And can write as good Latin or any other school language from 'Mother to Moses.'" However, if want of kindness in my letter is the reason why Cywydd y Farn is dropt, I am in no way concerned at it; let him know, with thanks and compliments, that he does me a special and notable piece of service. But if it be for want of notes, &c., surely he that could make the Cywydd can also write notes on it; and if the noise about is so far gone abroad as to raise a general expectation, I don't know but it may be advisable to print it, and even requisite in some measure. Now your crown (if you can find in your heart to part with it upon so trifling an occasion) and mine, and another of Mr. Hugh Williams, will compass it, and we may have it and some two more printed here, under my own eyes, at Salop, and afterwards equally divided betwixt us, to be disposed of at pleasure. As to our national indolence and contempt of our own language, we can but take one view of the state of letters. It is a melancholy consideration; so full of discouragement, that I choose to say no more of it.[6]

Owen kneeled before the rudimentary altar and led the congregation in the Lord's Prayer. The chapel was warming now and, as expected, the children began to fidget. Owen rotely and quickly proceeded, cognizant of the audible groanings of his stomach. The New Testament lesson was from Romans, Chapter 13, and the two concluding verses arrested him: "Let us walk honestly, as in the day; not in rioting and drunkenness, not in clambering and wantonness, not in strife and envying. But put ye on the Lord Jesus Christ, and make not provision for the flesh, to fulfil the lusts thereof."

---

6. Jones, *Poetical Works (Vol. II)*, 36–38.

Goronwy and Me

What a master is drink, he reflected. With sadness and revulsion, he recalled his many episodes of "rioting and drunkenness," the immolation of the flesh, and the resulting swearing and gambling. Here in Brunswick, he had avoided the debauched spectacles of his past, and he again prayed for strength. His intemperance was a sin, and the weight of it was unendurable. As he had written in "Cywydd y Farn Fawr":

> The sinner . . . with guilty crime oppressed,
> Bears on his brow the fears of hell confess'd.
> Behold him now—his guilty looks—I see
> His God condemns, and mercy's God is He;
> No joy for him, for him no heaven appears
> To bid him welcome from a vale of tears.
> Hark! Jesu's voice with awful terrors swell,
> It shakes even heaven, it shakes the nether hell:
> "Away ye cursed from my sight, retire
> Down to the depths of hell's eternal fire,
> Down to the realms of endless pain & night,
> Ye fiends accursed, from my angry sight
> Depart! For heaven with saintly inmates pure
> No crime can harbor or sin can endure,
> Away! Away where fiends infernal dwell,
> Down to your home and taste the pains of hell."

Returning his gaze to the devoutly kneeling congregation, Owen pronounced with a loud voice, "The Lord be with you." The worshippers answered, "And with thy spirit." The priest continued. "Let us pray. Lord have mercy upon us. Christ have mercy upon us. Lord have mercy upon us."

The Heartwells lived in Brunswick County for at least 250 years, and it is certainly possible that my great-great-great-great-great grandfather, Israel Heartwell, knew Goronwy Owen. Israel Heartwell was a planter who died in 1802 after a long life. His third son, and my lineal ancestor, Paul, was born in 1741. During the Revolutionary War, he was a captain in the county militia and may have been with Lafayette at Yorktown. What I know about these and other of my Heartwell progenitors comes from a little handmade booklet entitled *The Heartwell Family of Brunswick County, Virginia*. This document was "assembled and arranged" by Lucy Dorgan Heartwell, my mother, and my siblings and I justifiably consider it a treasure trove of family history. While it may not be exactly riveting, *The Heartwell Family of Brunswick County, Virginia* is certainly entertaining. Consider, for example,

November, 1763

some of the names hiding in the foliage of the family tree: Littleberry Heartwell, Saphronia Jane Heartwell, Horace Hilliard Heartwell, and Cinderella C. Solomon Heartwell among others. Now I know someone named Proal has no latitude when it comes to judging the monikers of others, but I find these family names worthy of bemusement, and, I suppose, admiration.

The Heartwell Family of Brunswick County, Virginia was created by Mother in 1983, way before "Ancestry.com." In her preface to the document, Mother, in her flowing script, explains to us the "motivation" of the project, as well as its "process."

> My dear children,
>
> Here is more than you ever needed to know about Heartwells! When I started this to occupy myself during the February of my foot recovery and in response to Buck's request for some basic Heartwell information, I had no idea that I had accumulated so much in the years that Heartwells, in one form or another, have been my primary concern and pleasure.
>
> The Tarver-Heartwell Bible which now belongs to your father was helpful. It was given to P. E. and C. C. Tarver, presumably when they were married. After the widow Tarver married Dr. Charles Paul Heartwell, they, then their son and his second wife and daughter made entries.
>
> I added the wives of the Heartwells as the last section so you'd have all connections together, and so I could close the books on ancestors. The rest of the search—and there are many unanswered questions—is up to you! Much of what I've put together could profit from your reevaluation.
>
> Finally, these are bare bones and as such may be disappointing to you. The stories that fleshed them out into real people are lost to us with the grandparents and cousins who knew them intimately. But look between the lines and, especially, consider the dates, and the situations and relationships take on more interest and meaning.
>
> Your families were amazing resilient and, ultimately, totally successful, because they produced you.
> Love to all,
> Mother

This letter is quintessential Mother: gracious, wise, and self-effacing.

So, back to Israel Heartwell. His will is dated December 10, 1796, and it is curious to me on a number of levels. First the spelling of the last name is inconsistent throughout. Sometimes, it's "Heartwell" with an "e," and sometimes it's "Hartwell" without an "e." This lack of uniformity apparently plagued my family for many generations. My grandmother, the unrepentant southerner, always insisted that "Hartwell" was the preferred and traditional spelling until a carpetbagger with the same name showed up in Brunswick County after the War Between the States, or the "Late Unpleasantness," as Granny referred to the conflict. At any rate, it was imperative that our family distinguish itself from this northern parasite and, hence, "Heartwell" with an "e" became the custom. This, of course, is patently false, but like most of Granny's stories, it is a colorful tale.

There is another element to the will that is less fanciful. As he prepared to meet his maker, Israel Heartwell bequeathed a number of slaves to his wife, children, and grandchildren, and this practice continued in successive generations until the Civil War. Of course, slavery is our great national sin, and I'm bothered that my family helped perpetuate this evil. I could speculate that Israel Heartwell and his descendents were benevolent masters who treated their chattel with kindness and affection. But even if true, that's beside the point. The slaves were chattel and no amount of rationalization can alter the truth. So, ultimately, I'm ashamed that my ancestors were slave holders, and at the risk of sounding overly presumptuous, I'd like to apologize for their (and my) culpability in this sin.

Israel Heartwell's will appears below:

> I Israel Heartwell . . . to my son John Heartwell my Negro boy Orange and one feather bed and furniture.
>
> To Grandson Armistead Heartwell Negroes . . . To Grandaughter Nancy Heartwell, the daughter of my son Paul Hartwell, Little Fanny, child of my Negro woman Amy.
>
> To my son Richard Hartwell, 5 shillings sterling
>
> To my son James, a Negro . . . To my beloved wife Hannah Hartwell, 3 Negroes . . . and one feather bed and furniture and all remainder not hereunto mentioned and after the death of the above mentioned, Negroes and all residue and remainder of my estate that I lent to my beloved wife to my son Paul Hartwell to him and his heirs forever.
>
> I appoint my son Paul Heartwell as my whole and sole executor.
> 10th December 1796   Israel Heartwell
> Witnesses:
> Edward Webb
> Armistead Hartwell
> Patsy Hartwell
> Harrison Heartwell   Probate 26th April 1802

November, 1763

One final thought regarding Israel Heartwell's will: What am I to make of the bequest to his granddaughter Nancy of "Little Fanny, child of my Negro Woman Amy"? The possessive pronoun "my" is troubling. Was Amy more than a servant, I wonder. Could "Little Fanny" be Israel Heartwell's child? It seems, at least, possible.

Paul Hartwell's will demonstrates that he took his inheritance and built upon it. Filed in 1804, just two years after his father's death, the will continues the practice of passing on human beings from one generation to the next:

> In the name of God Amen: 13th September 1804
>
> I Paul Hartwell of the County of Brunswick low in boddy but of sound mind and full recollection . . . I give and bequeath unto my son Harrison Hartwell the tract or tracts of land whereon I now live reserving to my beloved Mary Hartwell her lifetime on the said land to him and his heirs forever.
>
> Item I give and bequeath unto my son Armistead Hartwell the tract of land whereon he now lives and the Negroes he has in his possession that I formerly gave him to him and his heirs forever.
>
> Item I give and bequeath unto my Daughter Nancy Hartwell one Negro Girl by the name of [?] one bay horse by Diomed also a good riding chair or [?] at the price of sixty dollars to her and her heirs forever.
>
> Item I give and bequeath to my daughter Elizabeth Tarver one Negro Woman by the name of Sibley and her increase to her and her heirs forever.
>
> Item My will and desire is further that all my estate not herein given shall be equally divided amongst all my children to wit— Elizabeth, Armistead, Harrison, and Nancy Hartwell . . . Paul Hartwell
>
> Fred Lanier
> William Gholson
> Lewis Johnson   Item Armistead and Harrison Heartwell and Frederick Lanier, Executors

From my perspective, the most interesting will is that of Harrison Heartwell, the third child of Paul Hartwell. (Harrison was largely "Hartwell" in his father's will, but "Heartwell" in his own.) Harrison married Rebecca Jane Lightfoot in 1819. She was twenty years younger than he, and she bore nine children in sixteen years. Harrison died in 1856 and Rebecca survived him by almost twenty years. Harrison Heartwell's will begins,

Goronwy and Me

> In the name of God Amen. I, Harrison Heartwell of the County of Brunswick and State of Virginia, being of sound mind and a disposing memory and knowing it is appointed unto all men once to die, do make and ordain the following as my last will and testament, in manner and form following to wit: 1st. I hereby revoke all other wills heretofore made by me.

In the second paragraph, Harrison writes,

> I lend to my wife Rebecca J. Heartwell for and during her natural life the following property to wit: one third part of my slaves, one third of my horses, mules, cattle, hogs and sheep, one third part of plantation tools and utensils.

This sentence is troubling to me in that slaves—human beings—are grouped with the livestock and farm implements. The sad implication is that these negroes are considered no more than animals or other tools of labor. I also wonder exactly how many slaves are represented by "one third." Finally, I don't know what to make of the word "lend." Legally, does it have a different connotation than "give" or "bequeath"?

This will was executed in 1855, and in it Harrison uses the term "slave" as opposed to "negro," the word employed by his father and grandfather. It is a subtle distinction, I know, but one that perhaps reveals the attitude of the antebellum planter class on the cusp of the War.

Harrison presumably was a man of great wealth, if wealth can be measured by property. He gave his son H. J. a tract of land valued at $4,500, "that being the amount I paid for the same." (Keep in mind that almost one hundred years previously, Goronwy Owen paid 90 pounds for 400 acres.) To his son C. P. Heartwell, Harrison gave another tract of land, also valued at $4,500. His married daughters Saphronia and Antoinette each received $10,000 in cash, "being the proceeds of sale of slaves sold in Alabama." (So much for the benevolent master theory.) Son Horace H. Heartwell was given, "the tract of land on which I reside together with my Grist mill attached thereto (subject to the life right of my wife Rebecca J. Heartwell) valued at $5,000. I also give to my said son Horace H. Heartwell all the plantation tools not already lent my wife, together with 110 barrels of corn, 4000 pounds blade fodder, 100 bushels oats and 2000 pounds pork which I deem sufficient for one farming year."

Additionally, Harrison Heartwell gives to each child (with one exception) anywhere between one and ten named slaves, with values ranging from $100 to $800. Some of the names (and value) of these thirty plus slaves

November, 1763

are: Boykin ($700); Anna ($300); Caty ($400); Slowman ($600); Manerva and child Amanda ($250); and Man Davy ($800).

The exception to Harrison's "generosity" is John Algernon Heartwell, the youngest child. Consider the ninth paragraph of the will:

> Owing to the extravagant and somewhat thoughtless disposition evinced by my son John A. Heartwell in his early youth, I make the following provision which in my judgment will best promote his interest and welfare, I desire that the value of $9000 in negro property, and $1000 in cash be placed in the hands of my three sons H. J. Heartwell, C. P. Heartwell, and Horace H. Heartwell as trustees for his benefit—I desire further that none of the above named property be applied to any purpose without the knowledge of each of the aforesaid trustees. Should, however, my son John A. when he has reached a mature age, manifest a more careful and considerate disposition, then and in that event I authorize my sons H. J. Heartwell, C. P. Heartwell and Horace H. Heartwell (the aforenamed trustees) and hereby give them full powers, if in their judgment they deem it best, to make over to my son John A. Heartwell a full and lawful right to the above named property which they hold in trust, or so much of it as shall then be in their hands to him, and his heirs forever. In the execution of the above provision, I desire that a reasonable sum be given annually to my son John A. to defray expenses.

Often I have wondered exactly what offenses were committed by John A. "in his early youth." Was he a gambler, a drinker, or merely disrespectful to his father? And did he, I wonder, ever "manifest a more careful and considerate disposition" and receive his inheritance? (Although this question is likely moot given that the Civil War commenced five years after the writing of this will.) His transgressions must have been great, for in the remaining codicils of the will, Harrison is clear to exclude his youngest child, inserting such phrases as "except my son John A. Heartwell" and "all my children, except my son John." Perhaps like Goronwy Owen, John forgot the admonishments of Romans 13: "Let us walk honestly, as in the day; not in rioting and drunkenness, not in clambering and wantonness, not in strife and envying. But put ye on the Lord Jesus Christ, and make not provision for the flesh, to fulfil the lusts thereof."

From the simple pulpit, the Rev. Goronwy Owen scanned the faces of his congregation. What did they think of him, he wondered. For two years now, he had served as the shepherd of this small flock. He baptized, married, buried, and visited those who were sick in both mind and body. He preached the word of God as he understood it. Did they appreciate him, appreciate his fervor? He was a minister; his days as a poet were over, he felt sure. There was no muse for him in this land. Yet, what had become of his poems? He had tried to publish them in 1757, but to no avail. Lewis had deserted him then, and Owen had not the resources, financial or otherwise, to bring forth his works. What was to be his legacy? Would he be forgotten, here on this foreign shore of trees and wild groves? The words of his poem "Y Bardd Coch" came back to him:

> "I am no rarity, but rather a poor, insignificant mortal . . . Yet, being God's creation, He will use me well and not hinder my two vocations [priest and poet]. If I possess gifts of poesy, let them be dedicated to holy lays. Woe to futile poetry and more woe to its author. Fair Lord, as I am a minister, let me minister unimpeachably. If shepherding a flock is an honourable calling, then the shepherd's burdens are many. The day will break when I must face the Lord to answer for many a soul . . . Hear me and help me, Lord, to sustain my revered and yet frightened vocation."

Martha Simmons smiled at him, and in her eyes Owen detected a glimmer of—what? Pride? Approval? Encouragement? He drew a deep breath and began his sermon, taken from the Gospel appointed for this day. As St. Matthew relates, "And Jesus went into the temple of God, and cast out all of them that sold and bought in the temple, and overthrew the tables of the moneychangers, and the seats of them that sold doves, And said unto them, It is written, My house shall be called the house of prayer; but ye have made it a den of thieves." Yes, there were always those who profaned the Word, took what was holy and used it for their own gain.

In 1763, through the efforts of his friends in England, Owen's collected works were published in the volume *Y Diddanwch Teuluaidd*. It is possible that the poet never saw this book. The preface of the edition took the form of a letter from Lewis Morris "To William Parry, Esq., Deputy-Comptroller of His Majesty's Mint in the Tower of London, and Secretary to the Cymmrodorion Society." Morris had apparently forgiven Owen for the rantings of his infamous "Cywydd i Ddaiwl" and was once again advocating on his behalf:

November, 1763

> Sir,—The Book that comes to you along with this, to be presented to the Society, was lately put into my Hands by the Editor, Hugh Jones; who took the pains to make the Collection, and has been at the Expence of printing it for his own benefit. He owned himself incapable of writing an English Preface to it, and therefore desired me to do that office for him. And as many of his Subscribers understand both Languages, he apprehended that the Book would be more general, if the Introduction was written in English, though he is no great Admirer of the Language: And seeing that the Writers of the pieces it contains, are of the Cymmrodorion Society, as well as the Printer and the Publisher, I thought a Letter to you, giving an Account of the Work, might stand very well instead of the usual flourish of a Preface; for the Book entirely belongs to your Society. And as I have the Honour of being a Member, I hope I shall not be censured in giving my Opinion thereof, in compliance with his Request.
>
> He owns, that some things therein contained, are published without Leave of the Authors; but hopes to be forgiven, as he had no intention thereby of hurting any Man; but to do himself Service, and help the Sale of his Book. Those Pieces, as well as the rest, being to be met with in private hands in Manuscript all over the Country. As the Authors are still living, one in North America [Owen], and the others in Wales, we may conclude, that their Compositions come to us more correct than those of former Ages, or of the Ancients, that must have unavoidably suffered by bad Transcribers: And I believe that few Books have appeared so free from typographical Errors in our Language: Let the Poetry answer for itself.

In the course of several more pages, Morris goes on to extol the sublime qualities of the Welsh tongue and point out the distinctions, subtle and otherwise between Welsh and English. Morris concludes this letter with an unusual aphorism:

> After all that is said here, I cannot help thinking of an ill-natured Expression of a surly old Acquaintance of mine, who hath no Taste to this kind of Entertainment; That a Poet and a Dancingmaster, much resemble one another; One makes Words dance to Music, to please the Ear; and the other teaches the human Species to trot about, to please the Eye. But the Wise Man says, there is a time for all these things; and happy is the Man who can apply it with Discretion.[7]

---

7. Ibid., 271–78.

Goronwy and Me

"Amen." Owen concluded his sermon. In the pews below him, a few heads nodded, but from approbation or slumber, he could not discern. He was once again aware of the growling of his stomach, and he thought of the dinner that awaited him. He led the worshippers through the prayers for His Majesty and the royal family before dismissing the congregation with the comfortable words from Second Corinthians: "The grace of our Lord Jesus Christ, and the love of God, and the fellowship of the Holy Ghost, be with us all evermore."

Outside in the churchyard, Owen exchanged pleasantries with the adults, as the children, freed from their confinement, scampered among the bare trees. He enquired after the sick and made promises to visit when he could. The crowd began to disperse, and Owen contentedly mounted his horse and fell in beside the carriage of Thomas and Martha. The crisp fall air reminded him of Anglesey, but he did not dwell on that association. This was his home now; this was the "temple of God."

8

July, 1767

***FROM* CYWYDD MARWNAD MARGED MORYS
(ELEGY FOR MARGARET MORRIS)
by Goronwy Owen**

Many a hundred loaves for sustenance
Did she give, where there were needy children;
Of a hundred old people did she meet the need,
Never to any one did she deny a gift;
A fine gift for the sake of the supreme God,
The warm-hearted minister of God.
An incomparable woman was Marged
In their midst, for unstinting gifts . . . The advice of a Doctor was not sought
By the weak, or his medication;
Where there was need for balm, fittingly
Was it given; heaven rest her soul.

Goronwy and Me

THE SETTING SUN CAST a limpid glow through the open, west-facing window of the Rectory's study. In the failing light, the Rev. Goronwy Owen strained to read again the letter he was holding. The ever-present flies droned torpidly in the encroaching dusk, and, reflexively, he swatted at a mosquito, insects which plagued this land like an Old Testament curse.

Outside he heard his children playing by the stoop, vigilant for the evening's first fireflies. Soon, Joan would gather them up and bring them to receive their father's benediction before ushering them off to bed. Under the rafters, and despite the oppressive heat, the rigors of their daily exertions would ensure sleep, sleep Owen knew would elude him this night. Robert, now seventeen and the only surviving child of his union with Elin, had left before dinner for the Richardson household and their comely daughter, Sarah. He would not return until the moon was high.

Owen lifted himself from the rocking chair and lit the oil lantern on his desk. He sat at the broad plank surface, dipped a fresh quill into the inkpot, and began:

> Brunswick July 23, 1767
>
> Dear Friend,
>   Having commiserated with you on the death of your two estimable brothers, I am next obliged to tell you how it happened that I heard of the sad occurrences. In short, this is how it happened: you, apparently, wrote to a certain Wm. Parry of Middlesex in this country, over a hundred and forty miles from my home, and he, after a long delay, wrote to me. I acknowledged his letter but have up to now not heard a whisper from him. I fear some rogue to have destroyed my letter before handing it to Parry. There is here no Port as in your country; one must trust the first person known to be bound for a certain vicinity, and sometimes a letter may take nine months or a year before plodding 30 miles, and often it never reaches its destination...[1]

As reported by John Gwilym Jones in *Goronwy Owen's Virginian Adventure*, Owen was an "obsessive letter writer" and most of his epistles were addressed to the Morris brothers. In fact, in his introduction to *The Letters of Goronwy Owen (1723-1769), Newly Transcribed and Edited by J. H. Davies, M. A. (1924)*, Davies notes that the volume contains thirty-seven letters to Richard Morris, twenty-nine to William Morris, and three to Lewis Morris. Davies concludes his introduction by asserting that "[Owen's] letters as a

---

1. Jones, *Virginian Adventure*, 30.

whole give us a clear-cut view of an interesting and vivid personality. He had the gift of portraying in picturesque language the persons with whom he came into contact, and the moods through which he passed; he is in turn serious, learned or witty. In English he is occasionally tedious and verbose, but never so in Welsh. As a letter writer in the golden age of letter-writing he must always occupy a unique place in Welsh literature."[2]

So how did Goronwy Owen, with his humble background, come into the sphere of the cultured Morris family? The answer clearly lies with Mrs. Morris, "the mother of four sons, three of whom became eminent in the literary history of Wales." In *Cywyddau Goronwy Owen, With Introduction, Notes, and Vocabulary (1907)* by W. J. Gruffydd, M. A., the author states that Owen, when a young boy, became acquainted with Mrs. Morris and her sons Lewis and William. Mrs. Morris apparently recognized Owen's precociousness and encouraged him in his studies. Indeed, she prophesied great things for him. As Owen later wrote in a letter to Richard Morris:

> I was fond of running from the school at Llanallgo to Pentre Eiriannell [the Morris home] on a Saturday afternoon, and there I would be sure to have my fill of pieces of bread and honey, treacle, or butter, or any of the three I preferred, some paper to do my school exercises, and many other things, a penny in my pocket to go home, and a strict warning, on taking my leave, to learn my lesson well; so that whoever might then be alive would one day see me as a cleric of some consequence.[3]

When Mrs. Morris died, Owen wrote a laudatory elegiac poem about her; she was, according to the Rev. Robert Jones, an "extraordinary woman . . . charitable and kind." As Jones also states, "If the formation of the mind and character . . . be the mother's work, her sons bore high testimony to her worth by their life and conduct."[4]

As we have seen, Owen enjoyed a quixotic relationship with these eminent sons. In *The Development of Welsh Poetry (1936)* by H. I. Bell, the author writes that the great Welsh literary renascence of the 18th century centered around the Morris family of Anglesey. Lewis Morris was "a poet of some importance" and he and his brothers were enthusiastic students of Welsh language and literature. They collected manuscripts and copied

---

2. Davies, *Letters*, x.
3. Williams, *Goronwy Owen*, 11–13.
4. Jones, *Poetical Works (Vol. I)*, 58.

texts, and they provided patronage to several poets who used bardic names in imitation of the poets' names of the classical period.

Bell goes on to say that Goronwy Owen was the "chief discovery" of the Morris brothers. According to Bell, Owen's poetry is academic in nature, replete with archaic diction and obsolete words and expressions. His themes are often remote, but his work possesses imaginative power and there is a great range of melodic effect in his lines. As Bell maintains, the poems that most engage Owen's personal feelings "kindle with inner fire."[5]

In regard to Welsh poetry, Bell asserts that Owen enjoys the same status as does Milton in English poetry. W. J. Gruffydd echoes this assessment, stating that both Owen and Milton "sang of high enterprise, in a lofty and heroic strain . . . to a small audience." However, Gruffydd believes Owen was not in touch with his time and that "his work is as far removed as possible from that of his great friend and patron, Lewis Morys" who was a poet of the period and of its people.[6]

Having finished his letter, Owen took a fresh sheet of paper and placed it on the desk in front of him. He knew that this night, with remembrances of Lewis monopolizing his thoughts, afforded him an opportunity, an opportunity to render a fitting tribute to his friend and patron. But this tribute must sing, and its echoes must be heard in Môn. It had been ten years since Owen had composed a poem, having left, he thought, his Muse in England. But the memory of Lewis gave him confidence, and he was ambitious to begin. He would write his elegy incorporating all twenty-four meters of Welsh bardic poetry. If he could do it, the effort would surely memorialize Lewis, and Owen, forever. Owen adjusted the lamp flame and trimmed his quill. He stared at the blank paper and waited, waited for Lewis to speak to him.

Owen had already written two poems about Morris, the glowing "Cywydd i Lewis Morys" and the scathing "Cywydd i Ddiawl." The date of the former poem is uncertain, but as the Rev. Robert Jones states, "it has a loved and honored name around which the poet's thoughts richly cluster, and on which he expends the warmth of his heart." Jones goes on to write, "the praise, therefore, it bestows, is not the expression of a mere temporary feeling, but the language of an affectionate gratitude."[7] This "masterly and

---

5. Bell, *Welsh Poetry*, 117–24.
6. Gruffyd, *Cywyddau*, i–xii.
7. Jones, *Poetical Works (Vol. I)*, 51.

imperishable Awdl" was translated in the late 1800s by George Borrow, author of *Wild Wales*. An Englishman and gifted linguist, Borrow learned Welsh primarily because of his affection for Owen's poetry. In *Wild Wales*, Borrow details his experiences and observations while touring Wales on foot in 1854, a sojourn that included a visit to Owen's native parish of Llanfair Mathafarn Eithaf. Borrow's rendering of "Ode to Lewis Morris (From the Welsh of Goronwy Owen)" begins:

> Bright silver, gold of ruddy glow,
> And gemmy cups I would bestow
> My much beloved friends upon,
> I'd give them many a precious stone,
> Had I but competence thereto,
> And who beyond his means can go?
> Thou Lewis shouldst obtain the best,
> Dear Lewis, man of noblest breast;
> Of golden vessels had I store,
> Work of the blacksmith god of yore,
> Thou shouldst obtain the treasure fair,
> None worthier of it breathes the air.[8]

As we have seen, however, Owen seeks to bestow upon Morris a more perverse immortality in "Cywydd i Ddiawl" after a breach in their friendship:

> A man of lawless nature,
> A half-breed, between man and devil;
> He roars with rage, and utters oaths,
> And damns this whole world:
> There is destruction to all where he is
> And joy for all where he is not;
> He was feared as God in heaven
> Feared more than the devil ...

H. I. Bell calls "Cywydd i Ddiawl" a "masterpiece of invective and macabre humour."[9] The Rev. Robert Jones also acknowledges that the poem may be read thusly, but he believes the effort was "wrought in mere sportiveness—a kind of banter to excite the laughter of the social circle in which he [Owen] and his friend Lewis Morris were moving." Given Morris's angry denunciation of the poem and its author, Jones's interpretation

8. Borrow, "Ode," 1.
9. Bell, *Welsh Poetry*, 117–24.

seems far-fetched. Yet, he insists that Owen's esteem for his friend allows for no other assessment. And, as he goes on to write,

> To learn his estimate of the noble qualities of Lewis Morris, we must read the poem he wrote to his memory ["Marwnad Lewys Morys Yswain"]—the effusion that came warm from his heart, when their could be neither hope of reward or desire of applause to induce it; for, be it remembered, he was now among strangers in whose ears there would be no music in his native tongue. Thousands of miles, and a broad ocean, too, intervened between him and Wales, the land where his strains would be read and appreciated. It was hardly probable that the poem would ever reach there, and less probable that it would be published. Yet, notwithstanding all this, how exquisitely wrought are its strains, how full of gratitude, how replete with emotion! The sentiments it breathes are so tender, warm, and generous, as to warrant the assertion, that truer regrets, or more genuine sorrow, never welled from the depths of a human heart.[10]

Owen lifted his red-rimmed eyes from the manuscript in front of him. His fingers were stained with ink and his sweat-drenched shirt clung to his back. On the desk lay his pipe, still warm to the touch from the tobacco that had fueled his efforts. The marwnad needed work he knew, but he was proud of the elegy, part tribute, part confessional, but eternal he hoped. He had incorporated each of the twenty-four meters in the poem, and in a burst of inspiration, the first seven stanzas formed a "Cadwen," a chain of "englynion" linked together by making the word that terminates the former "englyn" the beginning of the succeeding one. Above, Owen could hear the boys rising with the sun's first rays. He gathered and secured the pages before him to be reviewed after sufficient rest. He bowed his head and silently gave thanks for the Holy Spirit that had surely sustained him through the long night. In time, Owen would send the elegy to Richard, and, God willing, his poem would be a shining testament to the man who was Lewis of Môn.

Consisting of some two hundred lines, "Marwnad Lewys Morys Yswain" first appeared in *Gwilym Howel's (q. v.) Almanac* in 1770; it is the only surviving poem of Owen's dozen years in Virginia. In my research, I had encountered glimpses of partial translations of the poem—the first

---

10. Jones, *Poetical Works (Vol. I)*, 219–21.

July, 1767

few lines on the program of the memorial dedication at St. Andrew's; a few lines describing Virginia in articles by Edwin Williams and in Gay Neale's book—but as a native of Brunswick County I was naturally curious to find a version of the entire poem in my mother (and only) tongue. Meandering around the internet produced no leads, so I resolved to appeal to librarians for help.

Via email, I first contact the Swem Library at the College of William and Mary. Reference librarian Hope Yelich quickly replies and informs me that the library possesses many materials pertaining to Owen. However, a cursory survey of the collection locates no English translation of the "Marwnad." I thank Hope for her efforts and mention that according to www.tourbrunswick.org, "The Friends of Wales in Williamsburg are currently (1999) working on a new translation of the poem Owen wrote in Brunswick County." I asked Hope if she knows of "The Friends of Wales" and on my behalf she later contacts Robert Jeffrey, who graciously agrees to entertain my enquiries.

I learn from Bob that he and David Jenkins, a former English professor at William and Mary, had once worked on a translation of the poem. In fact, I gather that Mr. Jenkins is an avid "Goronovian," and that he and Bob had often led pilgrimages to Owen's grave in Brunswick County. Bob informs that the translation project has been dormant for over a decade. Unfortunately, Bob writes, Professor Jenkins is now in a nursing home and suffering from dementia, but "poet Michael Mott and I are planning to review the translation and work to improve it, hopefully for publication in Poetry Wales."

I ask Bob if I can meet with him to discuss the poem and the inherent problems involved in its translation. He agrees, and we make plans to convene for lunch in Williamsburg in about a month's time.

Meanwhile, I run into my former neighbor Jack Robertson, who is the Foundation Librarian at Monticello's Jefferson Library. Jack does some "poking around" and soon emails me the following:

> I looked in the following online resources for "goronwy owen" (a delightfully distinctive two-word phrase so unlikely to be mistaken for anything irrelevant; however, I did discover that there are a number of individuals with that name!)
>
> Va. Historical Society (14 hits)
>
> OCLC WorldCat (141 hits, so I narrowed the search to "owen goronwy" as Subject=27 hits)

Goronwy and Me

> American Antiquarian Society (1 hit, the 1969 Botetourt publication, no. 2)

I explore the links Jack has sent me and many of the materials at the Historical Society are familiar ones. I look at the hits from WorldCat (the world's largest online library) and again discover listings for books and articles which are already known to me. However, I note that there are two citations for "Ode to Lewis Morris, from The Welsh of Goronwy Owen" by George Henry Borrow. I wonder if this ode bears some connection to the "Marwnad." (Later, of course, I learn that it does not.) When I click on these sites, I discover that this poem was printed in an edition of twenty copies, and that among other places, these volumes can be found in the libraries of Yale, Wesleyan, and Oberlin, as well as at the Pierpont Morgan Library in New York City. Jack submits an official interlibrary borrowing request for a photocopy (the document is only eight pages long) from the universities noted, and I anxiously await for what I hope will be good news.

I also contact Alison White, a friend who works at the Library of Congress, and I ask her for any advice she can offer regarding my hunt for the "Marwnad." She replies that she "did a very quick search in the Virginia Heritage database of finding aids for manuscript materials held in Virginia libraries and historical societies" and located records at the Swem Library and the Library of Virginia. Alison acknowledges that "it doesn't seem likely a translation of the poem would be in the above" but she vows to continue to search. An additional inquiry to the Digital Reference Section of the Library of Congress generates the following reply from Peter Armenti: "I have checked translation indexes, poetry indexes, biographical sources about Goronwy Owen's life, and collections of Owen's work and related criticism, but have been unable to find an English translation of 'Marwnad Lewys Morys Yswain.' My best suggestion for confirming that an English translation of the poem has not been made is to contact the National Library of Wales, which holds a collection of Owen's correspondence and literary papers."

I have, in fact, already contacted the National Library of Wales, and I soon receive a reply (in English and Welsh) from Lona Jones:

> Dear Mr. Heartwell,
>
> Thank you for your enquiry concerning Goronwy Owen's poem to Lewis Morris. I have not found an actual translation of it, but a heavily annotated Welsh version with English notes may be seen in the second volume [pp. 253–269] of Owen, Goronwy,

July, 1767

1723-1769? The poetical works of the Rev. Goronwy Owen (Goronwy Ddu o Fon): with his life and correspondence/edited, with notes, critical and explanatory by Robert Jones.

Peter Armenti from the Library of Congress had also referenced this book, which, of course, I own. It's beginning to look more and more that an English translation of the poem does not exist. Since it is unlikely I will ever learn to speak or read Welsh, I await for news regarding Jack's request for the George Borrow translation.

However, Jack's efforts elicit no responses, even after earnest and repeated attempts to obtain the desired poem. Consequently, one day I walk the two blocks from my school to the public library in search of its circulation manger, David Plunkett. David is a former student of mine at Charlottesville High School, and we often chat about what each of us is currently reading and our mutual affection for the works of William Faulkner. David's father has recently retired after a long stint as the director of special collections at the University of Virginia library. I explain my dilemma to David and ask him if he thinks his dad might have better luck than Jack acquiring a photocopy of the Borrow translation. "Perhaps," David replies, but he suggests instead that the public library put in a request for an interlibrary loan. He introduces me to reference librarian Noelle Funk who completes the necessary paperwork on my behalf and sends it off to Wesleyan University. Again, I retreat into waiting mode.

I do, however, make two quick trips to Richmond: one with Randy to the Library of Virginia, and one with Susie to the Virginia Historical Society. The purpose of these excursions is to peruse materials pertinent to Owen, and, perhaps, to discover a morsel or two relevant to the "Marwnad." I do not find any information on the poem, but I do glean additional tidbits about Owen and the efforts to keep his name and work alive. At the Library of Virginia, I discover an article entitled "Goronwy Owen and His Bicentenary" published in London by the Cymmrodorion Society in 1924. This article provides details of the January 18, 1924 unveiling of a commemorative tablet at St. Mary's Church, Northolt, Middlesex where Owen served as Curate-in-charge from 1755 to 1757, just prior to his departure for Virginia. The tablet reads:

> In Memory Of
> Goronwy Owen
> 1723–1769
> Curate Of This Parish

Goronwy and Me

> 1755–57
> Master Poet And Prose Writer
> In Whose Works
> The Ancient Dignity And Beauty
> Of The Welsh Language
> Shone Forth Anew
> This Tablet Was Erected
> By The Honourable Society
> Of Cymmrodorion
> 1923
> DYN DIDOL DINOD YDWYF
> AC I DIR MÔN ESTRON WYF

The program for the ceremony is published in the article "as a memento of the occasion." The order of events includes an opening hymn, the reading of a lesson from Ecclesiastes, and the unveiling of the memorial. This act is followed by three "tributes to the Genius of Goronwy Owen" and "Acknowledgements on Behalf of the Honourable Society of Cymmrodorion." Of course, I am interested to learn that these "acknowledgements" are delivered by the Chairman of the Council, the Rev. G. Hartwell (!) Jones, D. D., D. Litt. During the course of the ceremony, a letter from H. R. H. the Prince of Wales, Patron of the Society, is also read:

> I much regret that my engagements will not permit me, as Patron of the Honourable Society of Cymmrodorion, to join the Council in unveiling the Tablet which Dr. Pritchard, on their behalf, has set up in St. Mary's, Northolt, to commemorate the connection with that church in 1755–57 of the distinguished Welsh poet, Goronwy Owen, whose bicentenary we now celebrate. The tablet truly records that he was a "Master-Poet and Prose writer in whose works the ancient dignity and beauty of the Welsh language shone forth anew," for as Principal Davies, of the University College of Wales, justly observes in his recent book—The Letters of Goronwy Owen 1723–1769—"he introduced into Welsh Literature a new conception of poetic dignity and style and at the same time put new life into the traditional forms of poetic expression." I rejoice that a Society with which I am happy to be associated should pay this small tribute to the memory of a Poet who has so greatly enriched and added luster to his country's literature.

> (Signed) Edward P. [11]

---

11. *Y Cymmrodor*, "Bicentanary," 37–40.

While at the library, I also dabble with a genealogical database and discover that one Richard Hartwell, a minister from Liverpool left Bristol in 1750 to serve at Blanford Church, built in 1735. Blanford, located near Petersburg, Virginia and some forty miles from Brunswick County is where Goronwy Owen died in 1769. Apparently, the Rev. Hartwell's tenure at Blanford was short-lived, so it is unlikely he ministered to Owen in his decline. Today, Blanford Church is a memorial chapel and Confederate shrine in honor of 30,000 soldiers buried in its cemetery. The church features fifteen stain-glass windows donated as a memorial from each Confederate state, personally designed and executed by Louis Comfort Tiffany.

Susie and I explore the Owen "artifacts" at the Virginia Historical Society, and most interesting to me is a series of articles by the Rev. Edwin T. Williams that appeared in 1957 in the *Brunswick Times Gazette*. The articles provide details of Owen's life and the efforts of the Rev. Williams and others to perpetuate his memory. The first installment of the series chronicles plans for a festival in Owen's honor to be held the next year. This, of course, is the March, 1958 dedication ceremony of the memorial cross at St. Andrew's. This article also quotes J. Hudson Jones, secretary of the Saint David's society of the State of New York who comments, "Yes, the memory and story of Goronwy Owen in America are like a candle flame in the wind. It may flicker, but it will never die."[12]

With Owen's story still "flickering" in me, Susie and I set off for Williamsburg on a beautiful September Saturday morning. Our plan is to spend a couple of hours at the Swem Library on the campus of the College of William and Mary. Susie will then lunch with Elise's friend Emilia, now a student at William and Mary, while I rendezvous with Bob Jeffrey. At ten o'clock in the morning, the library is eerily quiet as Susie and I search for the plaque there that honors Owen. We locate it, snap a few photos, and skim through the books on the adjacent shelves which form a sort of Owen alcove. I make a few notes before we head off to the library's archival section, the catalogue of which details vast holdings of materials related to Owen and his years at the college. There is also an apparent portrait of the poet, which I request to see. When the framed rendering is brought forth, I have misgivings. The subject looks little like the dark-visaged writer ("Goronwy Dhu") of my imagination. There is much to explore, but as it is near my appointment time with Bob, further research at the Swem will have to wait.

12. Williams, "Flame," 1.

Goronwy and Me

I meet Bob at The Green Leafe and over an extended lunch we discuss Wales, the Welsh language, and the life and work of Goronwy Owen. Bob's great-grandparents came to Virginia from Caernarfon near Mt. Snowdon in Wales. They settled in Arvonia, a small community of Welsh slate miners in Buckingham County, not far from Charlottesville. Buckingham County is also the location of Bremo Bluff, the home of John Hartwell Cocke, a member of the first Board of Visitors at the University of Virginia. (The Board of Visitors also included James Madison and James Monroe.) As a young man, Bob learned snippets of Welsh from his father, uncles, great uncles and men who worked in the quarry. As Bob recounts, "After church, the men folk would gather in my great-uncle Dave Morgan's basement and smoke cigars and drink whiskey. Then the Welsh would begin to flow."

Bob refers me to several books which he thinks will illuminate my research, and he suggests places Susie and I should visit on a proposed trip to Wales in the summer of 2011. We talk about Owen's poetry, and, according to Bob, the "music" of the Welsh language gives Owen's work its beauty. Bob further notes that the poetry is "telescoped"; there is a sense of compression in that a massive story is told in a relatively small amount of lines. Through combinations of sound, beauty bursts forth from these stories. Bob asserts that Owen preferred to keep his life and his imagination separate. His poems often exhibit an enhanced sense of longing; he wrote more powerfully of Wales being absent from it. This separation, Bob claims, makes Owen's poetry successful.

According to Bob, the "Marwnad" is Owen's "show-off piece." The poem is architecturally complex and its language is difficult to translate as Owen resorts to anachronisms and "tortures syntax and substitutes sound for sense in order to fulfill the requirements of whatever bardic meter he's trying to replicate." Apparently it is also difficult to capture the poem's emotion. As H. I. Bell writes of "Cywydd y Farn Fawr," "it is impossible to give an English reader any real idea of its excellence which lie almost wholly in its style.[13]" Bob shares with me the "rough draft" of the translated "Marwnad" he and David Jenkins worked on years ago.

We talk further of my "project" and Bob tells me about his screenplay "Devilsburg," which explores the intersecting lives of Thomas Jefferson, Jacob Rowe, and Goronwy Owen. Bob gives me a copy of a DVD titled *O Fon I Virginia*, which was produced by the Welsh language affiliate of the BBC and was shown on BBC-Wales throughout the country. Bob was a

---

13. Bell, *Welsh Poetry*, 117–24.

July, 1767

consultant on this Welsh documentary about Owen's life in Virginia, and the film includes footage of Williamsburg and Brunswick County, including St. Andrew's and the shell that is Owen's house.

My time with Bob has been truly revelatory, and I'm appreciative of his generosity. My interest in Owen remains unabated, but I also realize how much I don't know. I wonder, not for the first time, where to draw the line. How much do I need to learn to satisfy my own curiosity? Is "total immersion" necessary, or even possible?

A few days after the trip to Williamsburg, I receive an email from Noelle at the Jefferson-Madison Regional Library. The requested "Ode to Lewis Morris" has arrived from the Wesleyan University Library. When I first read the poem, I suspect that it bears little relation to the "Marwnad." For one thing, the poem is considerably shorter than the roughly two hundred lines I had expected. Yet, there are two notes attached to the text that allow for a soupcon of possibility. As a preamble to the "Ode," Borrow writes, "Showing that there is nothing which better causes a man to be remembered after his death than the work of the bard, and that neither the sculptor nor painter can give such a portrait of a man as the poet can. After the manner of Horace, Lib. IV., Ode VIII, viii." Is Borrow suggesting that Owen wrote the "Ode" after Lewis Morris's death, or is he merely acknowledging that the poem helps perpetuate Morris's memory and reputation? My confusion is enhanced by "A Footnote to the Ode to Lewis Morris" which appears at the poem's conclusion. Written by Clement Shorter, an apparent friend or patron of George Borrow, the "footnote" is copied below:

> This poem is here happily associated with three famous men of letters, with George Borrow its translator, who obtained distinction through prose and not through verse, with Lewis Morris (1700–1765), and with his friend Goronwy Owen (1723–1769). Morris was a Welsh poet, philologist, and antiquary, who led for the most part the prosaic life of a Government land-surveyor. Forty years of his life were given up to a great historical dictionary entitled *Celtic Remains*, which was completed in 1760, but not published till more than a hundred years afterwards—in 1878. He greatly befriended the wayward Welsh poet Goronwy Owen, whom he described as "the chief bard of all Wales," and Goronwy, when he heard of his friend's death, wrote the ode here produced. Owen had been a schoolmaster and curate in England before he won distinction as a Welsh poet, carrying with his gift something of

Goronwy and Me

Robert Burns's weakness of will. He died in Virginia. Borrow has referred to him with enthusiasm in *Wild Wales*.[14]

Again, there is the assertion that the Ode was written after Morris died in 1765.

I send Bob Jeffrey a copy of the document, and his initial reply states, "The Borrow doesn't appear to me to bear any close relationship to the Welsh text of the Marwnad." A few days later he confirms that the poem Borrow translated is "Cywydd i Lewys Morys," a "different poem altogether than the 'Marwnad.'" He goes on to say, "looking through Goronwy's work, I see lots of poems that have not been translated, or not translated well." During the course of our email exchange, Bob also informs me that his good friend and co-translator of the "Marwnad," Professor Emeritus David Jenkins, has passed away. A number of his friends host a poetry reading in his honor in the Great Hall of the Wren Building, and Bob reads in Welsh some excerpts from the "Marwnad" at this event. Fourteen poets also participate, and, according to Bob, others send tributes and anecdotes to be shared. Bob concludes this account by stating, "We decided to spread some of David's ashes at the Goronwy gravesite in Brunswick County."

The exchange with Bob irrefutably confirms what the Library of Congress and the National Library of Wales had previously suggested: no published translation of the entire "Marwnad" exists.

As an undergraduate at the University of Virginia, I took a fiction writing class taught by John Casey, who was later to win the National Book Award in 1989 for his novel *Spartina*. A few years ago, John addressed a continuing education class on local writers that I was auditing. The subject of his presentation was his translation of the Italian novel *You're an Animal, Viskovitz!* by Alessandro Boffo. During the course of the lecture, John rather flippantly remarked, "A good translation is like a wife, either beautiful or faithful, but rarely both." Certainly as one who is linguistically challenged, I am in no position to discuss the nature of the art of translation. But I do trust that Bob, or perhaps someone else, will one day render "Marwnad Lewys Morys Yswain" into an English work that is both "faithful and beautiful."

Owen's muscles ached from his night's labor. He stepped from the house to feel the warmth of the sun as it rose above the circle of cedar trees in his yard. In the distance, he could hear Robert working along side

---

14. Borrow, "Ode," 4.

July, 1767

Stephen, pulling suckers from the broad green leaves of that tobacco that stood in neat rows in the southwest field of his property. Soon the crop would hang in the dark, weathered plank barn to cure before going to market. Its sale would supplement his salary from the parish, and the welcome monies would help him provide for the children and Joan, who was again with child.

Owen was content. Although far from his native land, in a strange and hostile place where he never spoke or heard the language he so loved, he had, through unstinting effort and unwavering faith, made a home. God had used him for His purposes, even though Owen knew he had not become, as Mrs. Morris once predicted, "a cleric of some consequence." But where would he be without the Morris family, he wondered. Their friendship, their patronage, their memory were manna for his body and soul, and he prayed that the "Marwnad," once finished, would safely find its way to Richard.

The Rev. Goronwy Owen turned back to the house. He would eat, wash, rest. But not for long. There was work to do.

9

June/July, 1769

**FROM AN ELEGIAC POEM IN MEMORY OF
THE REV. GORONWY OWEN
by Lewis Morris, Esq., of Penbryn**

What tho' an exile's grave
Holds thee; thou art blest. Great God, 'tis more
To have crept to the grave, to have crawled a slave from birth,
Leaving naught richer but the charnel earth,
Than, surfeit with gold, sodden with luxuries,
To pine in vain before heaven's close shut door;
More to have known indeed
The sweet creative pang; and to have heard
The accents of the gods, and climbed with pain,
As thou didst all thy journey; nor in vain,
But seen as thou didst on the summit white,
Lear rays, tho' broken, of th' eternal light,
And those dread gates open without a word
For the heart and knees that bleed.

June/July, 1769

IT HAD BEEN AN ill-advised trip, he knew. He had ignored his fever and his own disquietude in his eagerness to consult with John Simmons, his brother-in-law. John was a man of commerce and his past advice had well-served the Rev. Goronwy Owen; Owen now sought to mine Simmons's wisdom as the slate miners of his native Wales plumbed the earth. John would not refuse Owen, the husband of his much-beloved younger sister, and father of his niece and three nephews. Yes, John would instruct him, perhaps even give him the capital for a new enterprise. With a growing family, Owen needed money to supplement what he deemed to be his insufficient salary. True, his farm had prospered, but a planter's life was a chimerical one, subject to the vagaries of weather, ravenous insects, and enervated soil. But trees, trees surrounded him and populated his county in numbers too large to calculate, like the descendents of Abraham. The tall pines yielded straight planks so necessary in the construction of the growing colony. Only sixty miles to the north, Richmond was a burgeoning city radiating outwards from the banks of the James River. Saw mills, with new technology from Germany, were sprouting in the colony. With a saw mill on his property, Owen could transform his resources and those of others into an inheritance for his children. Robert could oversee such an operation, and, in time, God willing, his brothers could help him. Owen knew well the Lord's admonition about a rich man entering the kingdom of heaven, but he only wanted what was his. His salary had not increased during his years as Rector, and the Vestry had to be goaded to give him his due. At his insistence, they paid him for keeping and carrying to church the sacramental plate, reimbursed him for the wine, and compensated him with tobacco for shrinkage on the glebe allowance. He knew the charity of others extended only so far; in this land, a man had to make his own way.

But the journey to Blandford had weakened him as the oppressive sun stoked his fever. He lay ill, and despite John's ministrations and the doctor's leeches, Goronwy Owen was perilously close to death. In the canopied bed, Owen clutched his Book of Common Prayer and recited the familiar words had so often uttered to others:

> HEAR us, Almighty and most merciful God and Saviour; extend thy accustomed goodness to this thy servant who is grieved with sickness. Sanctify, we beseech thee, this thy fatherly correction to him; that the sense of his weakness may add strength to his faith, and seriousness to his repentance: That, if it shall be thy good pleasure to restore him to his former health, he may lead the residue of his life in thy fear, and to thy glory: or else, give him grace so to

Goronwy and Me

> take thy visitation, that, after this painful life ended, he may dwell with thee in life everlasting; through Jesus Christ our Lord. Amen.

On June 24, 1769, Goronwy Owen wrote his last letter. In it, he asked his wife to come to Blandford, bringing with her their two youngest children and leaving the other two with her parents. The letter was delivered by Daniel, one of the Simmons's family slaves, and, apparently, Joan, with Jane and Richard in tow, made haste to Blandford where Owen died early the next month. He was forty-six years old. In his will, dated July 3, he leaves all of his possessions to his wife. His worth at his death is estimated to be about three hundred pounds, which contrasts greatly with the poverty Owen knew as a young man. As W. D. Williams concludes in his book, *Goronwy Owen*, "This sum of money, however, is but small, as compared with the wealth of poetry with which he endowed his nation. It can be said of him, as he wrote of his old friend and patron, Lewis Morris, 'Whilst teachers of poets continue to be honoured, and gentle painstaking learning remains in earnest hearts; whilst the language and the blood of the Brython remain worthy, he shall have most earnest and deserved memorials.'"[1]

Goronwy Owen's body was transported back to Brunswick County, where he was buried on his plantation. The Rev. Arthur Gray writes of the search for the poet's gravesite in the article "Gronow Owen in America":

> In a sparsely settled region, surrounded by scrub pines and scanty corn stalks, there was a little cluster of vines and evergreens which had evidently been untouched by the hand of man for generations. The plow had left a plot a few feet in diameter, uncultivated through the years, because it contained human bones, and no rustic, be he black or white, would knowingly disturb those quiescent spirits.
>
> Two old cedars, had fallen side by side, with their tops to the east, as though, tired of standing so long at the heads of two graves, they would over the place where those they honored lay. All indications point to the conclusion that in this cluster, described in the deeds as a plot 12 feet square, and reserved forever, lay the bones of Gronow Owen. And by his side? Was it the Iona, who in a moment of weakness had joined her fortunes with those of the wild Welshman, unknown to the world as yet, but who with flashing eye and storming phrases had won her fair hand?[2]

1. Williams, *Goronwy Owen*, 71.
2. Gray, "Owen in America," 239–41.

June/July, 1769

As previously noted, in 1901 Dr. Lyon Tyler detailed the story of Goronwy Owen's life in Virginia in the *William and Mary Quarterly*. In his article, Dr. Tyler quotes extensively from an account written in 1892 for *The Columbia* by Dr. Whyte Glendower Owen, a great-grandson of the bard, which traces the lives of the poet's descendants. Of John Owen, born in Brunswick County, Dr. Owen writes that Goronwy's son "emigrated to North Carolina; of him we have no record." The majority of Dr. Owen's piece is dedicated to Richard Brown Owen, youngest son of Goronwy and Joan Simmons. Born in 1767, Richard was educated at the College of William and Mary. What must it have been like for the child of the banished instructor to matriculate at the school where his father experienced such ignominy? Surely there were those in Williamsburg who remembered the intemperate Welshman. (But perhaps not. According to J. E. Morpurgo, "Goronwy Owen's stay at the College was short and distinguished only for its turbulence. Almost unnoticed in his coming, while he stayed he was despised as a reeling buffoon; he left in disgrace—and was soon forgotten."[3]) In 1789, Richard married Susan Edwards and together they had eight children, seven boys and one girl. Richard died in 1825 in Claiborne, Alabama where "he was a merchant by occupation." Several of Richard's children led distinguished lives, including second son George W. Owen, who was born in Brunswick County in 1798, but who settled in Mobile and held a seat in Congress for several terms.

Franklin Lewis Owen, Richard's fifth son, was born in 1803, and he, too, settled in Mobile. According to Dr. Owen, Franklin "held several offices under the Federal government, among them collector of the port. He also engaged in mercantile pursuits. He was universally respected and beloved, and died in 1890." He and his wife, Elizabeth Maury of Tennessee, had six sons and one daughter. The eldest son, Richard B. Owen, was born in Mobile in 1828, and educated at the University of Alabama. He was an attorney and represented Mobile in the state legislature. He served in the Confederate army and raised a large family. Dr. Owen writes, "Richard B. Owen is a courtly gentleman of the old school, and the high estimation by which he is regarded by his fellows is evinced by the fact that he was continuously elected mayor of Mobile from 1879 to 1888, at which time he decided to retire to private life." Dr. Owen continues. "Had his life been cast on different lines he would doubtless have enriched the literature of

---

3. Morpurgo, "Royall Colledge," 125.

his country, for some of his fugitive pieces show the true poetic fire of his great ancestor."

Franklin's fourth son, Goronwy Owen, was born in 1834, and he too was educated at the University of Alabama. In 1857 he received the degree of M. D. from the University of Pennsylvania and made his home in Mobile. He served as a surgeon in the Confederate army during the Civil War, after which he was the chair of obstetrics at the Alabama Medical College.

Of Franklin's sixth son, the author writes only that "George W. Owen, born in 1838, was educated in Alabama and saw 'grim visaged war' as a soldier in the ranks of the Confederate Army." More on George W. Owen shortly.

Dr. Whyte Glendower Owen concludes his article in the following manner: "This terminates the history of the descendents of Goronwy Ddu o' Fon. Some of them have served their country 'in the forum and the camp'; others have distinguished themselves in the liberal professions, and all of them have been honorable, upright Southern men, commanding the respect and good will of the various communities in which their fates were cast."[4]

I do not know what led so many of Goronwy Owen's progeny to Mobile, Alabama. Perhaps they were attracted there by the fable of the Welsh Prince Madog ap Owain Gwynedd who, according to legend, set sail in 1170 and discovered America. In fact, a plaque at Rhos, near Llandudno, declares, "Prince Madoc [sic] sailed from here to Mobile, Alabama," and in Mobile there is a plaque confirming he got there. Madog never returned to Wales, nor did any of the crew from the thirteen vessels of the expedition. It is said that they settled in the New World. Subsequent explorers claim to have encountered Native American tribes with distinctly Welsh characteristics who allegedly were descendents of Madog and his companions. According to Jan Morris, author of *The Matter of Wales*, the Mandan in particular

> were said to be just like Welshmen. They fished from coracles, they buried their dead in Celtic mounds, they spoke a language that shared many words with Cymraeg: for example cum in Welsh, a valley, was koom in Mandan, prydferth, 'beautiful' in Welsh, was prydfa in Mandan, while the words hen (old), glas (blue), aber (a river mouth), mawr (big) and many more were claimed to be identical in both languages.[5]

4. Tyler, "Goronwy Owen," 156–60.
5. Morris, *Matter*, 320.

June/July, 1769

Morris continues, "British settlers on the American seaboard were thrilled by these suggestions, which became one of the great myths of the country, and Welsh origins became highly fashionable among the colonists. No less excited were Welsh patriots at home, who saw in the affair confirmation that they were one of the seminal nations of the earth." In fact, Morris relates, in 1792 the "Welsh literati of London" (my fellow brethren of the Cymmrodorion?) sponsored a Welsh traveler, John Evans, to go to America in search of the lost tribe. Unsuccessful in his quest, Evans died in New Orleans in 1798, and the Mandans were eventually wiped out "by smallpox and Sioux."

Morris concludes that this fable "is like a protracted allegory . . . of ancient Welsh impulses. Facing the open liberty of the sea from their always circumscribed homeland, the Welsh have habitually sailed away in search of foreign truths and advantages . . ."[6] Like Goronwy Owen, perhaps? Richard Brown Owen and Susan Edwards were likely led to Alabama by less romantic yearnings, but it is nonetheless curious to me that several of their children ended up in the same piece of real estate as the legendary Prince Madog.

According to Mother's family research, my ancestors, the Dorgans, settled in Mobile at roughly the same time as Goronwy Owen's descendents. Andrew Dorgan, my great-great-great grandfather, was a "sailing master" in the American Navy who, in 1813, was given the pilot rights to Mobile Bay Harbor in recognition of his valor during the War of 1812. Andrew Dorgan returned to his home in New York City where he married Mary Van Arsdale in 1828; in the early 1830s he returned to Mobile with his young family, and in the city directory of 1844 is "Andrew Dorgan, 37 Church St., pilot." It seems likely that Andrew Dorgan, ushering ships into the harbor, would be acquainted with Franklin Lewis Owen, collector of the port. Andrew's two brothers were also bar pilots, and the Dorgan family served Mobile Bay for many generations. Consider the letter reprinted below from the Mobile Press Register of July 11, 2009:

> Saluting Dorgan family's service
>
> In 1813, three patriotic brothers were rewarded for their exemplary service in the U. S. Navy during the War of 1812. The Dorgan brothers were the first Americans to be branched (licensed) as Mobile Bar Pilots.

---

6. Ibid., 321.

Goronwy and Me

> The brothers took up residence at Navy Cove on the Fort Morgan Peninsula. This small Baldwin County community eventually became known as Pilot Town.
>
> Although the men were brothers, they were also business competitors. The men maintained a watch on top of a high sand dune, scanning the horizon for the sails of a tall ship. When a vessel was spotted, a race would ensue. The pilot with the fastest boat won the job of navigating the ship across Dixey Bar into Mobile Bay.
>
> Competition among the pilots increased as the Port of Mobile grew and more pilots were branched. This led to the ending of the races out of Pilot Town in the 1840s, when the pilots began using larger boats stationed at the sea buoy.
>
> Due to the high cost of maintaining station boats, the 16 branched pilots combined their resources and formed the Mobile Bar Pilots Association in 1865.
>
> In the 196 years since Timothy, Andrew, and John Dorgan were branches, there has always been at least one Dorgan working as a Mobile Bar pilot. In all, 14 family members spanning six generations took up this seafaring career.
>
> Sadly, this long and distinguished family tradition will come to an end Monday, when Sidney Eugene "Skipper" Dorgan III retires. The members of the Mobile Bar Pilots would like to thank Capt. Dorgan and his predecessors for their outstanding service to the Port of Mobile.
>
> We would like to extend to Skipper a traditional maritime farewell: Godspeed, fair winds, and following seas.
> Capt. Kirk M. Barrett
> Spanish Fort

Remember George W. Owen, who saw "grim visaged war"? Records indicate that during the Civil War he served in the Mobile Cadets with Augustus Proal Dorgan, Andrew's son and my great-great grandfather. What I know of this Company comes from an anonymous manuscript (William S. Coker, Editor) titled *The Mobile Cadets, 1845–1945: A Century of Honor and Fidelity*. According to the unknown author, the Mobile Cadets were the South's first company to volunteer for the Civil War. He writes,

> After the evacuation of Fort Sumter excitement ran high, and a call for volunteers was momentarily expected. When President Davis issued his first call through the Governors of several States, Capt. Sands, who was in the telegraph office awaiting news from

Montgomery, immediately wired Gov. Moore: "The Mobile Cadets tender their services and are awaiting orders."[7]

The company received its orders on April 23, 1861, and set off for Montgomery, where they joined other companies from the state to form the Third Alabama Regiment. The author describes the departure from Mobile as a "gala day":

> What gay and gallant boys they were, the Mobile Cadets and Washington Light Infantry [another Mobile company]; the flower of our youths, first in fun and frolic, and ever foremost in fight. All were in the highest spirits, and there was no flinching in this hour of parting from friends, as there were none, in after days, in the hour of meeting the foe.[8]

Immediately after its organization, the "Third Alabama" left for Virginia, and for the next four years the Regiment was engaged in most major battles of the conflict, including Antietam, Gettysburg, the Wilderness, Cold Harbor, and Petersburg. The Regiment was at Appomattox when Lee surrendered. Of the 175 members of The Mobile Cadets Co. A, twenty-nine had been "disabled by wound and discharged"; thirty-four had been "killed or died from wounds"; thirteen were "in Federal prison"; and eight "in hospital and on sick-leave." Clearly, the "gay and gallant boys" had suffered greatly.

After tracing the history of Company A, the author of *The Mobile Cadets, 1845–1945* turns his attention to a second company formed in April, 1861, in anticipation of President Davis's next call for volunteers. One hundred and three officers and men enrolled in Mobile Cadets No. 2 (Co. "K") and joined the 21st Alabama Regiment. Augustus Proal Dorgan was appointed 2nd Lieutenant (third in command) of Co. K, and G. W. Owen was among the enlisted men. Within a year, the 21st Alabama was engaged at Shiloh, at the time the costliest battle in U. S. history with over 20,000 Union and Confederate troops killed, wounded, and missing. During the two-day fight, the 21st Alabama lost six color bearers and 200 men, killed and wounded, out of 650 engaged. Co. K of the Mobile Cadets lost six men and fifteen were wounded, including G. W. Owen. (Coincidentally, also wounded at Shiloh was James Warley, grandfather of my mother's mother.)

---

7. Coker (ed.), *Cadets*, 19.
8. Ibid., 20.

Goronwy and Me

Due to the pervasive casualties, the 21st Alabama Regiment was reorganized after the battle, and, as a result, Augustus Proal Dorgan was promoted to Captain of the Mobile Cadets, Co. "K." At this time, enlistment was also extended from "one year" to "for the war." It appears that the Regiment spent much of the remaining war in defense of Mobile Bay, which included a bloody engagement with Admiral Farragut ("Damn the torpedoes, full speed ahead!") in August of 1864.

At the war's conclusion, the 21st Alabama Regiment was paroled in Cuba, Mississippi, a small town near Meridian. The book provides an inventory of the members of the Mobile Cadets Co. "K" and "What Became of Them." Many, of course, were killed or wounded and discharged. Others were captured and unaccounted for. Augustus Proal Dorgan "resigned" from the Company. Concerning G. W. Owen, the following notation appears: "Rejected by surgeon but volunteered without pay—badly wounded at Shiloh & discharged—Afterward joined another Company."[9]

I don't know what became of George W. Owen after the War. Did he and my great-great grandfather ever see one another again? Perhaps they both attended Company reunions and participated in parades commemorating various anniversaries of events experienced by the Cadets. But in 1939, the year after he sent my mother off to college in Virginia, my grandfather, the grandson of Augustus Proal Dorgan, moved from Mobile to Biloxi, Mississippi.

Some time after Goronwy Owen's death, Richard Morris sent a letter from England:

> "To the Revd. Mr. Gronow Owen, At New Brunswick, Virginia
> If the Revd. Mr. Owen is dead, I pray a line from the person who opens this, with some account of him and his family, directed to Mr. Morris
> Navy Office, London"

As the Rev. Robert Jones writes, "This letter, touching as it is, elicited no response. Goronwy was probably in his grave." The Reverend Jones continues in the penultimate chapter of his biography:

> Some years later—Dr. Owen Pughe mentions 1798—a few friends, revering his memory, tried to obtain information of their illustrious countryman through his son Robert. They wrote to enquire of him about his father. But the reply indicated that the son had either become thoroughly Americanized, or that he deeply resented the

9. Ibid., 135.

conduct of the British people towards one whom in his life-time they ought to have cherished and honoured. Its purport was, "that before he gave the information he must first know who would pay him for it."[10]

---

10. Jones. *Poetical Works (Vol. II)*, 299–300.

PART III

Bro Goronwy
(The Land of Goronwy)

10

Môn

IN THE VALLEY OF THE ELWY
by Gerard Manley Hopkins

I remember a house where all were good
To me, God knows, deserving no such thing:
Comforting smell breathed at very entering,
Fetched fresh, as I suppose, off some sweet wood.
That cordial air made those kind people a hood
All over, as a bevy of eggs the mothering wing
Will, or mild nights the new morsels of Spring:
Why, it seemed of course; seemed of right it should.

Lovely the woods, waters, meadows, combes, vales,
All the air things wear that build this world of Wales;
Only the inmate does not correspond:
God, lover of souls, swaying considerate scales,
Complete thy creature dear O where it fails,
Being mighty a master, being a father and fond.

Goronwy and Me

WALES IS A SMALL country, about two hundred miles from north to south and seventy miles across at its widest. Yet, it is this smallness that defines Wales: culturally, historically, and politically. As Jan Morris points out in *A Writer's House in Wales*, her native land

> ... is a little like Tibet. Geographically, even historically, Tibet is undeniably part of the Chinese landmass, but its cultural identity is just as undeniably separate, and its people feel their religion, their language, their whole way of life to be threatened by the influx of Han Chinese from the east. Also analogous is what used to be called Palestine. Wales is about the same size as the Holy Land, and in many ways its modern history has not been unlike an ironic cross between the history of the Palestinian Arabs and the history of the Palestinian Jews. On the one hand the Welsh have had to resist, as the Arabs have, the incursion of a more advanced and confident people—foreigners to themselves, as the Jews were foreigners to the Arabs. On the other hand they have been fighting to sustain, like the Palestinian Jews, a proud and ancient culture against an unsympathetic majority.[1]

Morris elaborates further on this paradox in *The Matter of Wales: Epic Views of a Small Country*. Here, she declares,

> It is not easy to be Welsh. Old torments attend the condition, like curses from a Celtic fairy-tale. There is the Torment of the Confused Identity—when is a Welshman not a Welshman, are some more Welsh than others? There is the Torment of the Torn Tongue—the anxieties of a society ripped apart by love, scorn, longing or rejection of its native language and culture. There is the Torment of the Two Peoples—the ambivalence of the Anglo-Welsh relationship, bitter-sweet, love-hate, never altogether frank. And behind these conscious malaises there is the more elemental Angst, only half-realized in Wales, which oppresses all such minority peoples, Jews in their dispersal, blacks of the New World, exiled Palestinians, lonely Afrikaners—the yearning, profound and ineradicable, for their own inviolable place in the world.[2]

Ultimately, Morris concludes, she lives "in a Wales of my own, a Wales in the mind, grand with high memories, poignant with melancholy."[3]

---

1. Morris, *House*, 12–13.
2. Morris, *Matter*, 423.
3. Morris, *House*, 48.

For the past two years, I, too, have inhabited a "Wales in the mind" as I stalked the elusive Goronwy Owen. For the most part, my perceptions of Cymru were formed by reading, viewing films, and talking with folks of Welsh heritage here in Virginia. But on the morning of June 11, 2011, Susie and I sit in a waiting room at the port of Dublin, preparing to board a ferry to take us across the Irish Sea to Anglesey. We had landed in Dublin the day before, on the first part of our longest and most ambitious odyssey as a couple. The day was spent touring the sights of the city: Trinity College, the Guinness Brewery, the Jameson Distillery. It had been a beautiful though exhausting day, and this morning we eagerly wait for the *Jonathan Swift* to carry us to Holyhead, where we will pick up a car and begin our exploration of the bard's native land.

Susie immediately strikes up a conversation with a young couple with a small child, also waiting for the ferry. These Dubliners are setting off for a weekend visit to family in Wales, childhood home of Kathrin, the wife and mother. She is an attorney in Ireland, but learning of our mission, she reveals that her father is a writer "who loves all those bardic poets." Kathrin's husband, an Irishman and a scientist, confirms that his father-in-law can "chew your ear off about Goronwy Owen." As we all part to board the ferry, I feel that our sojourn is indeed off to an auspicious beginning.

In his Introduction to *Wild Wales: Its People, Language and Scenery*, George Borrow writes, "Wales is a country interesting in many respects, and deserving of more attention than it is hitherto met with." Consequently, in 1854, Borrow set off with his wife and daughter to explore this land of "men of genius," chief among them, in his estimation, Goronwy Owen. Borrow states, again in his Introduction, that Owen was "a learned and irreproachable minister of the Church of England, and one of the greatest poets of the last century, who after several narrow escapes from starvation both in England and Wales, died master of a paltry school at New Brunswick, in North America, sometime about the year 1780."[4]

Of course we now know that Borrow's assessment of Owen is partially flawed. Given his run-ins with both ecclesiastical and civil authority, I don't think anyone would characterize Owen as an "irreproachable minister." And while Owen briefly served as Master of the Grammar School at the College of William and Mary, nothing in my research suggests he formally taught during his nine years in Brunswick County, where he was buried in 1769.

4. Borrow, *Wild Wales*, 19–21.

Goronwy and Me

Yet Borrow's affection for Owen was strong, and his desire to visit the poet's native parish was chief among his reasons to journey to Wales. Visiting Owen's "postage stamp of native soil" (to borrow a phrase from William Faulkner) is, of course, my primary motivation for crossing the Atlantic. Now I am not a traveler; in fact, I generally prefer to confine my meanderings to a ten-mile radius of my living-room chair where I can gaze at the trees out the bay window when I look up from whatever book I am currently reading. I guess you could conclude that I live a bit of a sheltered life. But I tend to agree with Eudora Welty, who states in *One Writer's Beginnings*, "A sheltered life can be a daring life as well. For all serious daring starts from within."[5]

With one or two exceptions, I have never really planned an extended trip, and I have never in my fifty-six years strayed outside the continental United States. Therefore, as the idea of the trip begins to form, Susie and I appeal to my sister Alison for help. Though she has never been to Wales, Alison has sojourned many times to the United Kingdom (she is an unabashed Anglophile), and she possesses many good insights on the "dos and don'ts" of overseas travelling. I send Alison a list of sites associated with Owen and tell her we are thinking of investing two weeks in our journey. Soon Alison emails us a proposed itinerary which is, by her own admission, "heavy on history." Susie and I tinker with the tentative plan and come to a few conclusions, the chief of which is this is going to be one expensive "research outing."

Some of our subsequent decisions about the trip are fueled by my own travel anxieties. For example, we determine to fly out of Charlottesville and thus avoid, as much as possible, the stress of major airports. Additionally, we think it best to go to Dublin and take the ferry to Wales. Dublin is a shorter flight than the alternatives, and I do not relish the idea of picking up a car in London, Manchester, or Liverpool and motoring into Wales from the east. I know my first exposure to "left-side driving" is likely to be disconcerting, if not downright terrifying, and I reason that my indoctrination will fare better in rural Wales than in urban England.

As we continue to explore the itinerary, Susie and I amputate the southern leg of our proposed trip. Cardiff, Swansea, and the Gower Peninsula are severed for sites that are, with perhaps one exception more, well, "Welsh." Also jettisoned are layovers in Oswestry and Shrewsbury. While these English destinations have Goronwy connections, there seems to be little there

---

5. Welty, *Beginnings*, 114.

Môn

that today resonates with the poet's past. Ultimately, our final schedule is to include four nights in Anglesey, one in Betws-Y-Coed, one in Hay-on-Wye, and two in Aberystwyth before driving back to Holyhead, ferrying to Dublin, and flying home. So, on a January afternoon, Alison comes to Charlottesville and armed with the internet and our Master Card, she and Susie start exploring and booking flights, ferries, and accommodations.

Early in April, Susie and I travel to Williamsburg to have lunch with Bob Jeffrey. I update him on the status of my research, and he shares with me a printed email from his friend John Owen. Bob had written John on my behalf, seeking names of potential contacts in Anglesey. Shortly thereafter, I write to Dewi Jones in Benllech. According to John, Dewi "was something of a Goronwy Owen scholar," and he and his wife Magdalen had given John and his wife Mary "a marvelous tour" during a visit in 1993. In May, via an email attachment, I receive the following letter from Dewi Jones:

> Stangau 17 Maes Llydan Benllech Ynys Môn LL74 8RD May 2011
>
> Annwyl Proal a Susie Heartwell,
>
> Thank you for your interesting letter. That you are currently writing a book about Goronwy is certainly good news which will be much welcomed in Llanfair Mathafarn-eithaf, in Anglesey and in Wales. I shall be forwarding a copy of your letter to Miss Elizabeth Hughes tomorrow, a distant relation of Goronwy and a resident of Dafarn Goch. We shall then know what her feelings are.
>
> The places to visit would be:
> Dafarn Goch in Rhosfawr itself.
> Llanfair Mathafarn-eithaf church where there is a commemorative pulpit.
> The Goronwy Owen Memorial Hall / Neuadd Goffa Goronwy Owen.
> Ysgol Goronwy Owen / Goronwy Owen School (Primary) where I was headteacher for 15 years.
> To follow the path (roughly) which Goronwy took to the school and to Pentre Eiriannell, the home of the Morris Brothers and their mother Marged Morris who invariably gave Goronwy a slice of bread and honey.
>
> I presented a piece of wood on which Goronwy had carved the letters G. O., to Bangor Cathedral a few years ago. Now it seems to be lost.
>
> I hope you have a pleasant journey to Anglesey and a worthwhile stay in Bro Goronwy (the land of Goronwy), a term which is very well used. It was first used in the name of the Literary Society

Goronwy and Me

>(Cymdeithas Lenyddol Bro Goronwy,—still going strong) in 1901, and devised by a teacher in the old school.
>Yr eiddoch yn gywir, Dewi Jones

Needless to say, I am delighted by Dewi's response, and a subsequent email exchange procures his phone number and a pledge to show us the sights.

When the *Jonathan Swift* disgorges us in Holyhead, I indeed feel a bit like Lemuel Gulliver cast ashore in a strange land. Susie and I make our way to the Hertz counter where we had reserved a car for our visit. The car, a diesel-powered Vauxhall "Insignia" is bigger than we had anticipated, and it later becomes a source of consternation as we navigate the narrow roads of Wales. Nonetheless, we stow our suitcases in the "boot" and set off on the A55 the twenty miles across Anglesey towards Beaumaris and the Bishopgate House Hotel. While Susie absorbs the spectacular scenery, I continuously repeat what is to become my mantra for the next ten days: "Left side of the road. Left side of the road. Left side of the road." We eventually pull into the tight streets of Beaumaris where I immediately, and perhaps predictably, clip the right-hand mirror of a parked car. (Don't tell Hertz!) We find our way to the hotel parking lot and check into the room that is to be our home for the next four days.

Beaumaris is a beautiful coastal town, and our first order of business is to visit Beaumaris Castle, a World Heritage Site and a short walk from the Bishopgate House. Begun in 1295 but never completed, Beaumaris Castle is the last and largest of the fortresses built by Edward I to cement his conquest of North Wales. Described as "perhaps the most sophisticated example of medieval military architecture in Britain," the castle's scope and design, which features both an inner and outer wall, awe Susie and me. Of its construction, Jan Morris writes, "The records show that 400 masons, 2,000 quarrymen, 2,000 unskilled labourers and thirty smiths were employed in the building of Beaumaris in Môn—the equivalent, it is said, of 13 per cent of the entire London labour force: from the site of this castle an entire Welsh community was expelled, to be resettled in the new town of Newborough."[6] Equally inspiring on this clear day are the views from the castle across the Menai Strait to the Snowdonia Mountains, which seem to beckon us with promises of unknown allurements.

Susie and I return to our room about five o'clock that Saturday afternoon, tired from our day which had begun in Dublin so many hours

---

6. Morris, *Matter*, 69.

Môn

ago. On an impulse, I phone Dewi in hopes of setting up a meeting for Sunday, or, perhaps, Monday. When I reach him, Dewi surprises me by suggesting that Susie and I visit that evening. He gives me directions to a convenient meeting spot—a mere thirty minutes away—and with some trepidation, Susie and I set off again in the Insignia, which I have rechristened "Goronwy."

Sadly, however, I muddle Dewi's directions and we wait and wait next to a telephone kiosk in Pentraeth while Dewi expects us at the telephone booth in Benllech, three miles away. After a bit of anxious second-guessing, I call Dewi's house and his wife Magdalen steers me in the right direction. Almost an hour after our appointed rendezvous time, we locate Dewi, and after profuse apologies on my part, we follow him to his house a short distance away.

A quick aside about Dewi and Magdalen Jones. They are a gracious and warm couple who immediately embrace Susie and me and who seem to take a genuine interest in my "project." Magdalen offers us tea while Dewi shows me several of his books about Goronwy Owen as I fill him in on Owen's life in Brunswick County. Around seven o'clock in the evening we embark to explore Goronwy's home turf, Dewi driving.

Chapter 30 of *Wild Wales* begins, "The day after our expedition to Snowdon I and my family parted; they returning by railroad to Chester and Llangollen whilst I took a trip into Anglesey to visit the birthplace of the great poet Gronwy Owen, whose works I had read with enthusiasm in my early years." Borrow then provides a brief overview of Owen's life before detailing over the next two chapters his own excursion from Bangor to Llanfair Mathafarn Eithaf, Owen's native parish.

Borrow's first stop is at a post office on the outskirts of Bangor where he learns that his desired destination is some ten miles distant. When asked why he wishes to visit Llanfair, Borrow replies, "to see the birthplace of the great Gronwy Owen." His inquisitor is amazed:

> "Well," said the old man, "I have lived here a great many years, but never before did a Saxon call upon me, asking questions about Gronwy Owen or his birth-place. Immortality to his memory!"

Borrow receives detailed directions for his journey, crosses the Menai Bridge, and eventually makes his way to Pentraeth and the public-house "The White Horse." Here Borrow pauses for a pint of ale and engages

Goronwy and Me

lodging for the night before continuing his journey to Llanfair. There he encounters a miller who inquires after his errand:

> "Did you ever hear a sound of Gronwy Owen?" said I.
>
> "Frequently," said the miller; "I have frequently heard a sound of him. He was born close by in a house yonder," pointing to the south.
>
> "O yes, gentleman," said a nice-looking woman, who holding a little child by the hand was come to the house-door and was eagerly listening, "we have frequently heard speak of Gronwy Owen; there is much talk of him in these parts."

Borrow shares an afternoon meal with the miller—John Jones—and his family, during which they discuss Owen's poetry. Borrow declares that it took him three years to understand Owen's use of ancient Welsh measures. Jones replies,

> "I would not have afforded all that time to study the songs of Gronwy. However, it is well that some people should have time to study them. He was a great poet as I have been told, and is the glory of our land—but he was unfortunate; I have read his life in Welsh and part of his letters; and in doing so have shed tears."

After his meal, Borrow continues his journey with the miller by his side. They come first to Owen's boyhood church:

> The church stands low down the descent, not far distant from the sea. A little brook, called in the language of the country a frwd, washes its yard-wall on the south. It is a small edifice with no spire, but to the south-west there is a little stone erection rising from the roof, in which hangs a bell—there is a small porch looking to the south. With respect to its interior I can say nothing, the door being locked. It is probably like the outside, simple enough. It seemed to be about two hundred and fifty years old, and to be kept in tolerable repair. Simple as the edifice was, I looked with great emotion upon it; and could I do else, when I reflected that the greatest British poet of the last century had worshipped God within it, with his poor father and mother, when a boy?

Borrow and Jones part company, and the author next encounters a Spanish-speaking mason, building a house. After exchanging pleasantries, the mason instructs "a lad of about eighteen" to lead Borrow to Tafarn Goch, Owen's home.

> I walked to the back part of the house, which seemed to be a long mud cottage. After examining the back part I went in front, where I saw an aged woman with several children . . . she smiled and asked me what I wanted.
> I said that I had come to see the house of Gronwy. She did not understand me, for shaking her head she said that she had no English, and was rather deaf. Raising my voice to a very high tone I said:
> "Ty Gronwy!"
> A gleam of intelligence flashed now in her eyes.
> "Ty Gronwy," she said, "ah! I understand. Come in, sir."

The "aged woman" serves Borrow tea, and he learns that she is the grandmother of the five assembled children, one of whom, when asked, writes in Welsh that her name is "Ellen Jones, belonging from afar to Gronwy Owen." Borrow concludes,

> When I saw the name Ellen I had no doubt that the children were related to the illustrious Gronwy. Ellen is a very uncommon Welsh name, but it seems to have been a family name of the Owens; it was borne by an infant daughter of the poet whom he tenderly loved, and who died whilst he was toiling at Walton in Cheshire,—
> "Ellen, my darling,
> Who liest in the churchyard of Walton," says poor Gronwy in one of the most affecting elegies ever written.

Borrow soon leaves the house and again engages the Spanish-speaking mason in conversation. Then he begins to retrace his footsteps toward Pentraeth and "The White Horse." He writes,

> After walking some way, I turned round in order to take a last look of a place which had so much interest for me. The mill may be seen from a considerable distance; so may some of the scattered houses, and also the wood which surrounds the house of the illustrious Gronwy. Prosperity to Llanfair! and may many a pilgrimage be made to it of the same character as my own.[7]

The first stop of our "pilgrimage" is Ysgol Goronwy Owen where Dewi had served as headteacher or principal for fifteen years. In fact, I gather that he was instrumental in naming this primary school here in his home town. I ask him how many of the three hundred plus pupils spoke Welsh,

---

7. Borrow, *Wild Wales*, 179–98.

and he answers, "All of them, by the time they leave." We then move up the street to Neuadd Goffa Goronwy Owen, or the Goronwy Owen Memorial Hall where Susie, our expedition photographer, snaps a picture of a commemorative plaque through a glass pane of the locked front door.

We leave Benllech and continue our journey through the countryside to the lane to Dafarn Goch. My visit to Owen's home would come later, but given my already abysmal record of following directions, I make careful note of my surroundings as we drive to Llanfair Mathafarn Eithaf Church. The exterior of the church appears much as Borrow described it, but Dewi has obtained a key and we are able to go inside. The interior reminds me very much of St. Andrew's in Lawrenceville; indeed the size of both spaces seem similar, and both exude (to me) a sense of peace and familial warmth. We admire the Goronwy Owen pulpit before leaving and roughly retracing the path to Pentre Eiriannell, the Morris family home.

We stop to take note of the Morris Memorial, erected in 1944 by the Cymmrodorion Society, and the monument more recently dedicated in 2010. We continue on and park at a spot that provides a beautiful panoramic view of the Morris homestead. A pasture dotted with sheep gently slopes towards a large house surrounded by several stone outbuildings. A small inlet of Red Wharf Bay laps the shore near the house and around a forested point, the sea beckons. It is an incredibly beautiful spot, and I can understand why young Goronwy found it so inviting and hospitable.

Dewi and Magdalen show us other highlights of their neighborhood, including the home of Hugh Griffith, who won the Academy Award for Best Supporting Actor in the 1959 film *Ben-Hur*, and sites associated with the 1859 wreck of the Royal Charter off Moelfre. The Joneses are incredibly proud of their "neck of the woods," and they share stories and information with enthusiasm.

We repair to their home, and we decline their invitation to dinner. It is nine o'clock now, still our first day in Wales, and I am anxious about the prospect of driving in the dark, not knowing that it will remain light for quite some time yet. Susie and I motor back to the Bishopgate House without incident, and I reflect on our remarkable day. Forty-eight hours ago, I was at home in Charlottesville, sitting in my chair reading about Wales; the past three hours had found me walking in the footsteps of Goronwy Owen in this land of "men of genius."

Môn

In the first chapter of Volume II of *The Poetical Works of the Rev. Goronwy Owen with his Life and Correspondence*, the Rev. Robert Jones, B. A., describes Owen's childhood home in the following manner:

> Goronwy was born on the first day of the year 1722, in a remote and secluded part of Anglesea, Llanfair Mathafarn Eithaf. His father's cottage stood on the borders of a moor, near the high road leading from Pentraeth to Llanerchymedd. Anglesey, however beautiful it may have been in days when forests covered it from the Menai to its northernmost point, has at present but few attractions, either of loveliness or grandeur, if we except, indeed, the margin of its renowned strait between the bridge that so nobly spans its waters and the pleasantly situated town of Beaumaris, and the sea-coast near the South Stack lighthouse. The neighbourhood of Goronwy's home in no way differed from the general character of the island. In the far distance, indeed, might be seen the towering rocks of Caernarfon; but they were too remote to sway with effect the imagination of the youthful poet. The influence, therefore, which mountain scenery exercises over the poet's mind, aided but little in modeling that of Goronwy. He exemplified the truth of the adage: 'Poeta nascitur; non fit.'[8]

On the blustery morning of June 13, Susie and I leave Beaumaris to visit Goronwy's "father's cottage" in the "remote and secluded part of Anglesea." The day before I had called Elizabeth Hughes, caretaker of Dafarn Goch; of course, she knew of my interest in visiting, courtesy of Dewi, and she cordially agreed to receive Susie and me the next day. We find our way back to the lane that led to the house, and I maneuver the car down this path to "Tŷ Goronwy." Surrounded by fields, the house is certainly unimposing from the outside, but it appears sturdily constructed with thick stone walls. Miss Hughes actually lives in a bungalow next door, and here, she immediately welcomes us into her home. She has set out tea, and while Susie helps her gather a few items in the kitchen, I peruse a catalogue of pilgrims to Dafarn Goch, an inventory begun many years ago by an aunt of Miss Hughes. Now eighty-three, Miss Hughes is a member of the seventeenth generation of Owen's family to live at Dafarn Goch, descended, I gather, from Robert Gronow, the brother of Goronwy Owen's father. A retired nurse, Miss Hughes clearly has a passion for the poet, and her knowledge of him is exhaustive. I am intrigued to learn that she had visited Brunswick County in 1995; she even shows me a picture of her by the marker for Owen's grave.

---

8. Jones, *Poetical Works (Vol. II)*, 2–3.

Goronwy and Me

    After tea, we walk next door to "Tŷ Goronwy" itself. We stroll about the yard, and note the privy and a series of sheds. Miss Hughes points out an original window of the house, and, adjacent to it, a patch in the dwelling's exterior finish where young Goronwy had carved his initials.

    We next enter the house, which, according to Miss Hughes, had been renovated in 1962. The interior walls are now covered with wood paneling, a necessary concession to combat peeling wallpaper caused by seeping moisture from the stone structure. The house is certainly a shrine to all things Goronwy Owen; laid out on tables in the downstairs rooms are framed letters, illustrations, and other memorabilia. I'm interested in a facsimile of Owen's family tree and the many books that adorn the cluttered surfaces. There are several "souvenirs" from the New World, including photographs of Williamsburg and familiar printed material on the poet's life.

    I am excited and honored to view all this "Goronovia," and it is such a joy to meet Miss Hughes. She is utterly charming and gracious; the twinkle in her eye gives her a youthful countenance that belies her advanced years, and I wonder what will happen to this house in the future. Here on just our third day in Anglesey, this visit to Dafarn Goch promises to be the highlight of our trip as I have inhabited, however briefly, the home that nurtured Goronwy Owen. Susie and I embrace Miss Hughes and bid her farewell. As we slowly drive down the lane to the highway, I recall the first two lines of Gerard Manley Hopkins' 1918 poem, In the Valley of Elwy: "I remember a house where all were good / To me, God knows, deserving no such thing..."

11

Cymru

WHAT PASSES AND ENDURES
by John Ceiriog Hughes

    Still do the great mountains stay,
    And the winds above them roar;
    There is heard at break of day
    Songs of shepherds as before.
    Daisies as before yet grow
    Round the foot of hill and rock;
    Over these old mountains, though,
    A new shepherd drives his flock.

    To the customs of old Wales
    Changes come from year to year;
    Every generation fails,
    One has gone, the next is here.
    After a lifetime tempest-tossed
    Alun Mabon is no more,
    But the language is not lost
    And the old songs yet endure.

Goronwy and Me

DURING OUR STAY IN Beaumaris, Susie and I stray from Anglesey on three separate occasions. Our first jaunt off the island is to Bangor on a very rainy Sunday, the second full day of our trip. The previous day had been bright and sunny, but when Sunday dawns, a cold rain saturates the landscape. As Jan Morris writes, ". . . the water of Wales . . . is ubiquitous. Millions of tons of it pour out of the heavens. This is one of the wettest corners of Europe, and the rainfall annals are full of proud statistics: at Llyn Glaslyn in Gwynedd 246 inches fell in 1922, ten times the London rate, while at Cowbridge, Pontfaen, in Glamorgan, in 1880, the heavens opened one day to deposit 2.9 inches in 30 minutes, the greatest half-hour load of rain ever recorded in Britain. Wales is soaked in rain, and its uplands spout with a myriad springs, and squelch with numberless morasses."[1]

Still, despite the day's "ubiquitous" rainfall, we climb into our car to drive the scant seven miles to Bangor and its cathedral, where I have learned there is a monument of some kind to Goronwy Owen. I have already determined not to visit Friars School, where free places were reserved for poor children like Goronwy on the condition they "promised faithfully to attend church on Sundays and holy days." Friars School was established in 1557 and designed to provide a classical education in Latin and Greek to its male students. However, the school had relocated in 1789, so I do not imagine there are remnants of Goronwy's tenure at the current site.

According to W. D. Williams, author of *Goronwy Owen* [1951], the young scholar remained at Friars School until he was nineteen years old. While there, "Goronwy, like everyone else, would regularly attend the services at the cathedral, clad in his white surplice, but it appears that his mind would sometimes wander away from the service, because he cut his name into one of the church benches, and that particular piece of wood has survived to this day."[2]

Is this the same piece of wood, I wonder, that Dewi refers to in his letter to me? The same piece of wood he presented to the cathedral a few years ago, but now "seems to be lost"?

Bangor is not a particularly big city, and I do not think it will be difficult to find the cathedral, which has been in continuous use longer than any cathedral in Britain. Yet, as we cross the Menai Bridge and enter the town, we cannot seem to locate what I imagine is a massive edifice. We drive round and round the University of Bangor and what appear to be

---

1. Morris, *Matter*, 17.
2. Williams, *Goronwy Owen*, 15.

several main streets, all to no avail. We even stop at a local grocery store for help and promptly get lost trying to follow the directions we receive. Finally, with nerves on edge from the pouring rain and our apparent aimless wanderings, I pull into a parking garage in the center of the city. When we exit on foot to the street, there immediately in front of us looms Bangor Cathedral.

Susie and I walk around the cathedral and come to the entrance only to find it locked. A pleasant fellow walking by informs us the church will reopen in about an hour. Susie and I set off to find a coffee shop, and we each enjoy a hot latte, which is remarkably soothing after our harrowing morning. In time, we return to the cathedral, and when we walk in, I am awed by the spacious white-walled interior. The cathedral is empty, save for the gentleman we had encountered earlier. He is apparently the sexton, and he is busy trimming candles and polishing brass in preparation of Evensong. He does not know of Goronwy Owen or a monument in his honor, but he encourages us to study the many, many plaques affixed to the walls.

We start poking about when suddenly we are enveloped by a wave, indeed a tsunami of sound from the organ. In the empty cathedral, music from the organist's rehearsal crashes about us with a volume I have never experienced in my years of church attendance. To me, it sounds like he is playing what could be the soundtrack to Goronwy's poem "The Day of Judgment" as the intensity of the piece feels as if could easily call forth heavenly multitudes. With this music as a backdrop, I finally find in a small side chapel a plaque in honor of Goronwy Owen. I can't read it—it is written in Latin—but I recognize his name and the Roman numerals suggest familiar dates. Susie takes a picture of the plaque and later that night she emails the photo to Laurie Duncan, Latin teacher at Village School. As requested, Laurie quickly responds with the following translation:

> Sacred to the deceased
> The venerable G. Owen, Master of Arts emeritus at the College of Jesus at Oxford,
> The most celebrated poet of our age,
> Who was born on the island of Mona in the year 1722
> steeped in nearly every good literature,
> he refined, improved, enriched
> His father tongue with the most devoted love
> This same man, whom well deserving in regards to his literature and homeland
> No patron however found delight

Goronwy and Me

> Nor was any protector welcoming,
> And because his own people rejected him
> Seeking to pour forth among foreigners
> In transatlantic lands
> He lived obscurely, died unknown.
> And lest the memory of such a man utterly decay,
> let this whatever-you-will be his monument.
> The men of Mona and certain other "lovers-of-the-muses"
> took care of the placement
> In 1831.

The text of the plaque is interesting to me in that it states Owen was "Master of Arts emeritus at the College of Jesus at Oxford." We now know that this is not true, and given his relationship with Lewis Morris, I am also surprised by the lines, "No patron however found delight/Nor was any protector welcoming." However, it does seem fair to conclude, "In transatlantic lands/He lived obscurely, died unknown."

Before leaving the cathedral, I pick up an information brochure by the door. In it, the following history is provided:

> About the year 525AD a man of noble birth named Deiniol settled on this site. Having been given land, probably by Maelgwn, King of Gwynedd, he enclosed with a fence constructed by driving poles into the ground and weaving branches into between them. The native technical term for this type of fence was 'bangor.' Within the enclosure Deiniol built his church. He and his followers erected huts or cells in which to live. They were missionaries, going about to evangelise and encouraging others to join them. All who came, individuals and families, built their own dwelling places and all would worship together in the little church. Thus a Celtic monastery or Clas was formed. As sometimes happens, the word 'bangor' was transferred from the original object—in this case the fence—to that closely associated with it—the settlement within. That is how Bangor got its name.

Also included in the brochure is the following: "Please take a few moments in saying this prayer before you leave us. Lord, forgive what we have been, amend what we are, and make us what we should be; for your name's sake. Amen."

Given my impatient attitude on the morning drive, this prayer request seems eminently reasonable, and I do as instructed.

Cymru

Susie and I make our way back to Beaumaris. The rain has eased now, and we set out on foot to further explore at host town. We discover a great restaurant—The Pier House—and enjoy a relaxing meal. Later, in the hotel bar, I sample my first taste of Penderyn, a Welsh single malt whisky, and the stresses of the day ooze away.

The next afternoon, after visiting Elizabeth Hughes, Susie and I drive to Conwy, a walled town that surrounds another of Edward I's castles. It is a lovely afternoon, and we opt not to tour the castle; instead we spend a couple of pleasant hours walking the city's hilly streets. We visit the smallest house in Great Britain and wonder how many times its last inhabitant, a six foot, three inch tall fisherman, banged his head on the low door header. At a local wine shop, I buy a bottle of Penderyn to fortify myself against any further onslaught of cold, wet weather. According to its website, Penderyn was "launched" in 2004. Its distillery is in the foothills of Brecon Beacons and there one cask of malted barley spirit is produced each day. I further learn that whisky distillation in Wales traces its roots to the fourth century and that one of the first commercial distilleries was owned by the family of Evan Williams who later immigrated to Kentucky to produce bourbon on the banks of the Ohio River. In the late 1800s, legal distillation was banned in Wales, primarily because of the temperance fervor associated with the rise of Methodism. This ban was in effect for over one hundred years. In the late afternoon we drive back to Beaumaris, where we enjoy another nice meal at The Pier House.

We are up early the next morning and off to Llanberis where we have booked seats on the Snowdon Mountain Railway. Britain's only rack and pinion railway, this train transports sightseers five miles to the summit of Mt. Snowdon, the second highest peak in the United Kingdom. Of Snowdon, Jan Morris writes, "That noble peak . . . is only 3,500 feet high, and you could easily fit the whole landscape, its rocky eminences, its winding river, its woods and its salt-flats, into one of the lesser Alpine glaciers. It is a dream view. It is as though everything is refracted by the pale, moist quality of the air, so that we see the mountain through a lens, heightened or dramatized."[3]

However, on this day it is warm and sunny, not "moist," as we begin our ascent. With the bright sun overhead, we are surprised to learn that it had snowed at the summit just three days ago. This is King Arthur's home,

---

3. Morris, *Matter*, 12.

or so it is claimed, and stories also link Merlin to the region. From our glass-enclosed railway car, I have no problem imagining knights and wizards peopling the cascading hills. We are surrounded by stone walls and rock, "the substance of Welsh nature," according to Morris.

At a steady five miles an hour, the climb to the summit takes the prescribed sixty minutes. We disembark for a short hike to the mountain's peak where, in a fit of hyperbole, the engineer has claimed we can see five kingdoms: Wales, England, Scotland, Ireland, and Heaven. After a half hour, we board the train again for our trip down the mountain. The views are indeed spectacular, and we observe many hikers on the trails leading to and from the summit. With his fondness for walking, I wonder if Goronwy Owen ever trekked these paths in his youth.

We return to Beaumaris before following the coast a few miles to Penmon ("head of Môn") to explore Penmon Priory and Puffin Island. It has been another full day absorbing the beauty that is Wales.

According to *The Rough Guide to Wales*, "Sprawled out across a flat plain around the confluence of the Conwy, Llugwy, and Lledr valleys, Betws-Y-Coed should be the perfect base for exploring Snowdonia." The guide continues: "Its riverside setting, overlooked by the conifer-clad slopes of the Gwydyr Forest Park, is undeniably appealing, and the town boasts the best selection of hotels and guesthouses in the region, but after an hour mooching around the outdoor equipment shops and drinking tea you are left wondering what to do."[4] Despite this less than enthusiastic endorsement, Susie and I had picked Betws-Y-Coed as the next destination in our Wales excursion. Accordingly, we leave Beaumaris (and Anglesey) behind on Wednesday morning and drive the narrow roads to Gorphwysfa House, our B & B for the night. Our room is not quite ready when we arrive, so we park our car and walk towards the center of town. *The Rough Guide* is right: there is a plethora of guesthouses and outdoor adventure shops. The town is beautiful, but I am a bit surprised how touristy this "gateway to Snowdonia" feels. As the Guide suggests, we "mooch around" and drink coffee (not tea) before heading back to Gorphwysfa House. We settle in and admire the toy railroad that traverses the yard before heading back to town to locate a trail head for a hike through the forest. The hour and a half walk takes us high above the town and affords us sweeping views of the river and valley below. It feels good to enjoy this natural setting first-hand and not from behind the

---

4. Le Nevez, et al., *Rough Guide*, 359.

Cymru

windshield of a moving car. We complete our hike and return to the B & B with sandwiches for an early dinner. Afterwards, we further explore on foot the neighborhood before retiring for the evening.

> In *Sixpence House: Lost in a Town of Books*, Paul Collins writes,
>
> Hay-on-Wye... is The Town of Books. This is because it has fifteen hundred inhabitants, five churches, four grocers, two newsagents, one post office... and forty bookstores. Antiquarian bookstores, no less. And they are in antiquarian buildings: there are scarcely any buildings in Hay proper that are under a hundred years old; not many, even, that are under two hundred years old. There are easily several million books secreted away in these stores and in outlying barns around the town; thousands of books for every man, woman, child, and sheepdog—first editions of Wodehouse, 1920s books in Swahili, 1970s books on macramé, pirated Amsterdam editions of Benjamin Franklin's treatise on electricity, and maybe even a few unpulped copies of John Major's autobiography.[5]

Susie and I are book lovers, so despite the fact that Hay-on-Wye has no connection to Goronwy Owen, we are eager to visit this town that straddles the border of England and Wales. The drive from Betws-Y-Coed is the longest of our trip—three and a half hours—and the route features many small towns, a few stretches of major highway, and lots of sheep. (Did you know that fifteen percent of all sheep in the European Common Market live in Wales, but only one percent of the people?) We find our way to St. Mary's B & B and begin our exploration of this village along the Wye River.

In *Sixpence House*, Paul Collins observes that, "Books are the cellars of civilization: when cultures crumble away, their books remain out of sheer stupid solidity. We see their accumulated pages, and marvel—what readers they were!" Yet Collins points out that Americans have never been voracious readers and/or buyers of books. In fact, he notes that "A recent survey found that half of American households did not buy a single book in the previous year."[6]

Remarkably, at the conclusion of a full afternoon canvassing the many book shops, Susie and I have not purchased a single book. We are, perhaps, victims of too many choices. What do you buy when there is no limit to your options? At each shop, I do dutifully ask about books pertaining to

---

5. Collins, *Sixpence*, 22–23.
6. Ibid., 2–4.

Goronwy and Me

Goronwy Owen, but my inquiries turn up no volumes of interest. We visit, among others, Hay Castle Books, Addyman Books, Hay Cinema Bookshop, and The Poetry Bookshop. Yet our favorite venue is Richard Booth's Bookshop, which houses approximately half a million tomes. In 1977, Booth "declared" Hay-on-Wye independent of the U. K. and appointed himself king. He created the wildly popular "Guardian Hay Festival" which, according to *The Rough Guide to Wales*, former attendee Bill Clinton called the "Woodstock of the mind." Apparently, Booth no longer owns his eponymous store; it is, however, a fascinating place. As Paul Collins suggests, ". . . the great thing about Booth's is that it is full of stuff that won't sell in a thousand years. You need to keep your ratio of the utterly obscure and the instantly familiar in careful balance: have too much of one or the other, and bankruptcy or insipidness is sure to follow. You need some odd "worthless" books because, like bending back lines to a vanishing point in a painting, the vanishing recognizability of a few titles in your stock gives the whole selection an appearance of depth."[7]

I enjoy rambling through Booth's, our last stop of the day, and I even chat with one of the booksellers about contemporary Welsh poets. Yet we leave the shop empty-handed before stopping by a pub for dinner and a locally-brewed beer.

The next morning finds us on the road to Aberystwyth. We eschew further book browsing in order to get ahead of the severe weather forecast for the mid-coast later that afternoon. Indeed the trip is rainy and windy, but we find our B & B without too much difficulty. Glyn Garth House is just a few paces from the Promenade, which buffers Aberystwyth from the sea. Ever the intrepid travelers, we wrap our rain gear around us, hold our hats to our heads, and start trekking through the city. We pause for lunch at The Treehouse Café, before continuing the steady climb to Penglais Hill and the imposing National Library of Wales. From the front steps of this building, dedicated in 1937, there is a spectacular view of the city and the coast. Susie and I enter the building and have mug shots taken for library cards that will grant us access to the reading rooms. In the South Reading Room, I do an online search of library holdings on Goronwy Owen which yields seventy-five hits. I peruse the entries for a bit, but unfortunately for me, all the holdings are in Welsh. We leave the reading room and stroll through a couple of exhibits, including one on the history of the King James

---

7. Ibid., 118.

Bible. We examine a copy of "William Morgan's Bible," which, according to Jan Morris, is thusly named "after the farmer's son who did much of the translation while rector of Llanrhaeadr-yn-Mochnant in the back-country of Clwyd, and whose humble birthplace among the forests of Penmachno in Gwynedd, is now a national shrine." Morris continues: "It was not only a work of religious devotion, religious expediency too: it was a miracle of literary revival. It created a standard Welsh prose, which drew upon the best traditions of Welsh writing, and permanently affected the manners and standards of the language."[8] We pause at the gift shop where Susie is excited to see works by Mari Eluned, a jeweler she has previously contacted and who we are planning to visit on our drive from Aberystwyth to Holyhead.

We leave the library, bow our heads into the wind, and once in town follow the meandering Promenade past the towering Welsh University College. Built in 1872, the construction of this institution was primarily funded by thousands of small contributions from the Welsh people and remains a source of pride to them. Indeed, as Jan Morris asserts, "old Aberystwyth students have a special affection" for this Gothic structure, "and whenever they walk along a seaside promenade, anywhere in the world, they still kick the railing at the end of the cornice, as they were accustomed to on their student walks from the College by the Sea, discussing the social implications of Unitarianism perhaps, or the poems of Goronwy Owen, through the winds off the wide Welsh bay."[9]

The next day we are up early for a morning walk along the Promenade. The rain has abated, but the wind still blows briskly. We walk to the railroad station where we catch the Vale of Rheidol Railway, an antique steam train that puffs its way about twelve miles to Devil's Bridge, or Pont ar Fynach. The sun is out now, and we opt to sit in the open observation car which affords unimpeded views of the unfolding lush landscape as we climb into the hills. At the terminus, we disembark and take a short hike to the Punch Bowl, so named because of a series of rock depressions gouged out by the cascading River Mynach. We return to the train and begin our descent to the city.

Back in Aberystwyth, we head towards Constitution Hill which rises sharply to a height of 430 feet from the northern end of the Promenade. After a steady climb to the summit, we enter an octagonal building that houses the world's largest camera obscura, a device that provides panoramic

8. Morris, *Matter*, 104.
9. Ibid., 243.

close-ups of the city, the mountains, and the bay. The wind is howling now, and I almost lose Susie to sea when she steps out on the building's deck to snap a photo. Before leaving the promontory, we chuckle at the sight of a nine-hole Frisbee golf course on this hill of raging wind and sheer drops to the churning water below.

We have enjoyed our time in Aberystwyth, a diverse and lively city that claims to be the home of more books per capita than anywhere in the world. (Richard Booth might quibble with this assertion.) But the next day is Sunday, our last in Wales. We are to drive to Holyhead, return our car, and catch the ferry back to Dublin for our Monday morning flight home. We leave Glyn Garth House right after breakfast and head north, detouring slightly to Mari Eluned's house between Dinas Mawddwy and Mallwyd. Mari crafts her jewelry out of pieces of slate. Before our trip, Susie admired Mari's work on her website, and she has asked her to make two necklaces she could purchase. Here, in person, the pieces are beautiful, and Susie does buy them both, one for her and one for Elise. Also, Susie has brought Mari a few small pieces of slate from Buckingham County, Virginia, which she had gathered in April during a day trip we took to the town of Arvonia. Around 1870, brothers Evan R. and John R. Williams, natives of Caernarvonshire, settled in Buckingham County, and through unstinting labor soon owned the slate quarries there. Shortly thereafter, more Welsh immigrants arrived—including Robert O. Jeffrey, Bob's great-grandfather—and the area where they settled was named Arfon, from "a 'r Fon" or "the land across from Môn." Arfon was later Anglicized to Arvon, which, in time, became Arvonia. Today the settlement's small cemetery is replete with headstones featuring Welsh inscriptions. Courtesy of Gen. T. S. Jeffrey, Bob's late uncle, a Welsh flag flies above the entrance of this walled graveyard. There is still an active quarry in Arvonia today, and its slate is considered some of the finest in the world. Mari's home is surrounded by slate hills, and it is not far from Porthmadog, formerly the chief exporting port of the Welsh slate trade.

We leave Mari's home and find our way back to Holyhead where we manage to get on an earlier ferry for our return to Dublin. The next morning Susie and I set off for the airport where we endure a day of indignities likely familiar to travelers more seasoned than we. Our time in Wales has been transformative, and I feel its beauty and hospitality is now an indelible part of me. I have learned much about Goronwy, and I better understand the influences that shaped his life and work.

12

Hiraeth

IN A MIAMI BOOKSHOP
by David Greenslade

> I'll find it
> for you
> on the screen
> where did you say it was
> between the great slave cities
> Liverpool and Bristol
> not Edinburgh
> that's in Scotland
> London is less than three hours away
> no problem
> they still speak their language there
> is that right
> but you can't
> you can only say 'thank you'
> in it
> yet you insist
> that it's a country
> that's quaint

Goronwy and Me

this language
has nothing in common
with English
you don't know anything else about it
too bad
your two most famous drunks
both died away from there
struggling for perspective
from the lees
of their biography
as if that background mattered
there's nothing listed
under Mabinogion
try coal
try druids
try Princess Di
no other image springs to mind
there's nothing here
no bagpipes
no Knoxville Highland Games
no famine
staining Boston green
no traditional ethnic shame
to lacerate a grandchild's hand
try Seltic
you say Keltic
tell me again
spell it
say it plainly
Where did you say you were from?

Hiraeth

SHORTLY AFTER OUR RETURN to Charlottesville, I receive the following letter:

>Lluest Wen
>>Breeze Hill
>>Benllech
>>Ynys Môn
>>LL74 8UB
>>11 June 2011
>>Dear Proal Heartwell,
>>CYMDEITHAS HANES BRO GRONWY
>>BRO GORONWY HISTORICAL SOCIETY
>
>>I learn from my friend Dewi that you are currently writing a book on Goronwy Owen's life in Virginia in his later days. This was mentioned in the Committee of the above society recently and the members were united in wishing you well with the project. You are of course aware that we are very proud of the poet who was born and bred in this locality.
>>I hope that you enjoyed your visit to Anglesey and to Bro Goronwy.
>>Yours sincerely,
>>Myra Jones (Secretary)

The letter is a sincere and sweet gesture, and it serves to further motivate as I continue to work on "the project." Yet the missive also stirs up a bit of trepidation. What if my writing fails to do justice to the poet who is, even today, such a source of pride to those of his native "locality"? Or, what if my conclusions about him cast him in an unflattering light? Well, for better or worse, this marks the last chapter of my narrative, and any reader who makes it this far can draw his or her own conclusions about Goronwy Owen.

What indeed are my final thoughts regarding the poet and clergyman? Well, clearly he was an enigmatic person, a man of many contradictions, who in his lifetime and since, inspired in others conflicting emotions. These paradoxes occur in assessments of his demeanor, his temperament, and his body of work. Even his physical appearance seems at odds with itself, as he is variously described as "stocky" or "slender and lithe." Apparently, he was capable of great affection, but full of invective which he often unleashed on his closest associates and friends. He was a man of great conviction and piety who through his own weakness of character experienced degradation and despair. In other words, he was human, and like all humans, he was deeply flawed. And finally, as Branwen Jarvis writes, "he failed to reconcile inner hopes and longings with outward circumstances."[1]

So, beyond the obvious facts of his life, what did I learn during these two years of self-imposed Goronwy mania? Well, first of all, I learned that I am, at best, a serendipitous scholar. While I enjoyed researching the poet's story, I do not possess the resources of time and intellectual acumen to fully do him justice. My work has been more anecdotal in nature and that is fine with me. Someone else will one day produce the definitive work (in English?) on the contrary Welshman. But I also discovered how revelatory and rewarding even modified research can be. For example, in addition to gaining an appreciation of Owen's life, I, through my meandering explorations, found new writers to admire, enhanced my understanding of poetry and language, made new friends, and learned about a part of the world with which I was totally unfamiliar. Most importantly, perhaps, I learned about my own home and the life my ancestors forged there. I have not lived in Brunswick County for many, many years and aside from brief excursions, have no desire to ever return there. Yet, I am grateful for the role of this place and its people in ineffably making me who I am today.

I also learned, or rather confirmed, that the line between myth and reality is often a blurry one. During the past two years, I have been amazed by the inconsistencies and misrepresentations of Owen's story. Some of these errors can be attributed to a lack of information, but others, I suspect, are more willful in nature, or at least, reflect the practice of filtering facts through a lens of one's own design. Certainly, Owen's tale confirms the axiom that history depends on who is telling it.

I come away from the experience of writing this narrative awed by the passion Owen still inspires in others. For many, he still lives and breathes, and his life is a source of constant re-examination and speculation. Why it was even suggested to me that Owen might have been the child of Lewis Morris! Now, I hate to glibly toss in this rumor, but you have to admit, it is interesting to consider. Remember that Siân Parri, Goronwy's mother worked in the household of Marged Morris, and that Lewis Morris was about twenty-one years-old when Goronwy was born. Might there not have been an attraction between the cultivated Morris and the young mother who was, according to her son, always "careful to correct an uncouth, inelegant phrase or vicious pronunciation"?[2] And what of Morris's ardent

1. Jarvis, *Goronwy Owen*, 2.
2. Williams, *Goronwy Owen*, 9.

Hiraeth

and unflagging support of Owen throughout the younger poet's lifetime? Morris taught Goronwy about poetry and encouraged him in his craft. He supported him financially and worked fervently to bring Owen's poems to publication. Even after the rift perpetuated by "Cywydd i Ddiawl," Morris, like the father in the parable of the prodigal son, slaughtered the fatted calf for Owen. And what of Owen's "Marwnad" for Morris? The elegy is effusive in its celebration of the Lion of Môn. Well, who knows.

Perhaps the best lesson I've gleaned is that it is important to know when to call it quits. There is still much to learn about Owen and his work, but for me, "enough is enough." I know a lot about Goronwy Owen. To learn more would require that I study Welsh so that I could better appreciate his poetry. My understanding of the "ancient bardic meters" is superficial at best. I can explain what the cywydd is, but without an understanding of the Welsh language, I cannot fully appreciate its complex rhythm. As Jan Morris points out, "the rules of [Welsh poesy] and the sounds of the Welsh tongue are made specifically for each other."[3]

And what about that Welsh tongue? Native Welsh speakers insist their language is entirely logical in its construction and pronunciation. Undoubtedly, they are correct, but as they suggest, maybe English speakers struggle with Welsh because their tongues are not long enough! Or, as Jan Morris explains,

> Most foreigners find Welsh the very devil to learn, largely because it uses a phonetic device called mutation, under which the initial letters of words are often changed by gender, or by the last letter of the word that came before: For instance the Welsh word for "head" is "pen," but "my head" is "Fy mhen." It has several letters, too, that are not in the English alphabet: "dd" which sounds like "th" in "thin," "ff" which is the English "f," "ll" which is rather like the English "thl," and "ch" as in Johann Sebastian. All this means that until you have mastered the alphabet, and learnt the complex rules of mutation, a dictionary can be maddeningly unhelpful.[4]

For me, Welsh, as Paul Collins observes, "is a form of cipher, like German Enigma machines—none of the letters is pronounced the same as the letter would indicate to an English speaker."[5] Though I will never master

---

3. Morris, *Matter*, 152.
4. Morris, *House*, 142.
5. Collins, *Sixpence*, 128–29.

Welsh, I love listening to it, and I am glad Wales is experiencing a revival of interest in its language, one of the oldest in Europe.

So what is Goronwy Owen's legacy today? Certainly there are physical memorials to his memory; let's review them. In Anglesey, there is the primary school and the community hall in Benllech, living testimonials to the poet's memory, if you will. And, of course, let's not forget Dafarn Goch, the poet's childhood home. There is the plaque at Bangor Cathedral, erected in 1831 by "the men of Mona," as well as the statue at the University of Wales, Bangor. There is the commemorative tablet unveiled in 1924 at St. Mary's Church, Northolt, Middlesex, where Owen served for two years before departing to Virginia. In Virginia, there is the 1957 plaque in the Swem Library at The College of William and Mary, and, of course, the Celtic cross in Lawrenceville funded by the Poetry Society of Virginia and dedicated on March 2, 1958. And if you look hard enough, you can still find the skeletal remains of Owen's Brunswick County home and a marker denoting his gravesite.

But the real legacy of Goronwy Owen is his poetry and the passion and pride it engenders in the Welsh people. His poems, and the prose of his surviving letters, are vibrant, tangible links to the country's literary traditions. Today, these traditions are celebrated in events and festivals like the annual eisteddfod, or "a meeting of the bards." His legacy lives on in the revival of interest in the Welsh language, a movement which would surely hearten the man who claimed Cymraeg was equipped "to express the sublimest thoughts, and in as sublime a manner as any other language is capable of reaching to."[6] And then there are the books about Owen, the most recent and comprehensive published in 1997, as well as at least one documentary film and a couple of screenplays awaiting production.

So it appears that Goronwy Owen's legacy is secure and will surely survive, whether or not my own contribution ever sees the light of day. I have enjoyed getting to know Goronwy Owen and discovering those things which we have in common. Indeed, I have made a new friend in Goronwy and, as in all enduring friendships, I am, undoubtedly, a better man because of our acquaintance.

Let's close our narrative with "An Elegiac Poem in Memory of the Rev. Goronwy Owen" by Lewis Morris, Esq., of Penbryn, a great-grandson of Lewis Morris, friend, benefactor, and muse of Goronwy Owen. This poem appeared in the first volume of *Y Cymmrodor* or *Transactions of the*

---

6. Jones, *Poetical Works (Vol. II)*, 52.

Cymmrodorion Society. According to the Rev. Robert Jones, Morris "repays with an admirable elegiac poem the elegiac poem that Goronwy wrote to his talented relative's memory."[7]

> Friend, dead and gone so long!
> Was it not well with thee, while yet thy tread
> Gladdened this much-loved land of thine and ours?
> Came not thy footsteps sometimes through life's flowers?
> Knew'st thou no crown but that which bears the thorn?
> Amid the careless crowd, obscure, forlorn;
> Who sittest now among the blessed dead
> Crowned with immortal song?
>
> A humble peasant boy,
> Reared amid penury through youth's fair years,
> The fugitive joys of youth thou didst despise,
> Ease, sport, the kindling glance of maiden's eyes;
> Thou knew'st no other longing but desire,
> With young lips parching with the sacred fire,
> To drink deep draughts of knowledge mixed with tears—
> A dear-bought innocent joy.
>
>
> The treasure-house of Time
> Lay open to thy young and passionate thought:
> The bard who sang the tale of Troy divine,
> The tragic pomps, the Athenian fancies fine,
> The stately Roman marching to the swell
> Of his own verse,—all these thou lovedst well;
> And yet it was no one of these that taught
> The secret of thy rhyme.
>
> For to the ancient tongue
> Thou didst attune thy lyre. Thou hadst no choice
> To what fair measures thou shouldst fit thy song,
> But to the bardic numbers sweet and strong,
> The old melodious Cymric accents deep,

7. Ibid., 309.

Goronwy and Me

Didst wed the winged thoughts that might not sleep,
Singing as sings the thrush, with clearer voice
Than ever bard had sung.

And for a fitting meed
What was't thy country gave thee? Thou didst give
Thy life to serve the Master; yet didst ask
No high reward or guerdon for thy task,
No alien mitre for thy patriot head,
Only assurance of thy children's bread,
The things that perish for the words that live,—
'Twas a poor wage indeed!

Yet not even this was thine;
The great ones of thy land took little heed
For souls like thine, pent by the vulgar crowd;
Hungering for pelf and place with clamour loud,
What care had peer or prelate for thy lays?
Thou wouldst not stoop to crown with venal praise
Souls gross with pride and sunk in vulgar greed,
Through thy sweet verse divine.

Then hope deferred too long
Sickening the heart—the bard's too sensitive brain—
Then seizing thee, drove thee at last to seek
Oblivion of the pain thou couldst not speak,
Forgetfulness of failure, brief surcease
Of long solicitudes, which is not peace!
There is a joy with deadlier tooth than pain,
A self-inflicted wrong!

And hadst thou then no friend
To mark, to chide, to cherish, and to praise?
Aye! one thou hadst, whose dear and honoured name
Gains added luster from thy greater fame,
Who knew the voice of genius, and who knew

Hiraeth

The long steep path between it and its due;
He with wise bounty smoothed the anxious days
Which only death might end.

And thou, bright soul, in turn,
Didst with such grateful song thy friend requite,
That through all future days of bards to be
He lives immortal in thy Elegy;
He lives a poet in a poet's verse
Whose praises still his country shall rehearse,
When in high congress, 'in the eye of light,'
The bardic accents burn.

Two poets from one isle,
The greater thou, and he, though great, the less,
'The Lion of Mona.' In the ranks of song
Learning nor fame avails; nought but the strong
Sweet inspiration which the rapt soul knows,
When the fire of heaven the swift lyre glows
And wakes the strain which joyless lives shall bless,
Making life's desert smile.

What though thy pitiless lot
Drove thee an exile o'er the Atlantic sea,
Far, far, from thy beloved land, and set
Where alien fortunes lured thee to forget
Thy too cold mother; yet thy soul would yearn
For thy dear Wales,—unchanged thy verse would burn
In the old tongue thy birthright gave to thee—
Sweet sounds unforgot!

What though an exile's grave
Holds thee, yet thou art blest. Great God! Is it more
To have crept to the grave, to have crawled a slave from birth,
Leaving nought richer but the charnel-earth,
A lump of grosser clay, rotten with ease,

Goronwy and Me

Surfeit with gold, sodden with luxuries,
And pine in vain before heaven's close shut door
Bearing no pain to save?

Than to have known indeed
The sweet creative pang; and to have heard
The accents of the gods; and climbed with pain,
As thou didst all thy journey,—nor in vain,
But seen as thou didst, on the summits white
Clear rays, though broken, of the Eternal light,
And those dread gates open without a word
For the heart and knees that bleed?

Rest, tranquil, happy ghost;
Thou art blest indeed, whate'er thy earthly ills!
The wordlings who once passed thee in life's race
Lie in dishonor; no man knows their place,
Faded and gone; their very names have fled;
No memory keeps the undistinguished dead;
Thy fame still green thy grateful country fills—
Fame never to be lost!

Bibliography

Bell, Edith Rathbun, and William Lightfoot Heartwell, Jr. *Brunswick Story*. Printed and Published by Brunswick Times-Gazette, Lawrenceville, Virginia, 1957.
Bell, H. I. *The Development of Welsh Poetry*. Oxford: The Clarendon Press, 1936.
Borrow, George. "Ode to Lewis Morris: From the Welsh of Goronwy Owen." Reproduced from the original in Special Collections & Archives, Wesleyan University Library.
———. *Wild Wales: Its People, Language, and Scenery*. London: J. Murray, 1868.
Chambers, S. Allen. "Of the Best Quality: Buckingham Slate." *Virginia Cavalcade* Volume 38, (Spring, 1989): 158-171.
Coker, William S., ed. *The Mobile Cadets, 1845-1945: A Century of Honor and Fidelity* (Anonymous Manuscript). Bagdad, Florida: Patagonia Press, 1993.
Collins, Paul. *Sixpence House: Lost in a Town of Books*. New York: Bloomsbury, 2003.
Davies, Hywel M. "Goronwy Owen, the Parsons' Cause and The College of William and Mary in Virginia." *Transactions of the Honourable Society of Cymmrodorion (1994)*: 40-64.
Davies, J. H., M. A. *The Letters of Goronwy Owen (1723-1769), Newly Transcribed and Edited*. Cardiff: William Lewis (Printers) Ltd., 1924.
"Goronwy Owen and His Bicentenary." *The Transactions of the Honourable Society of Cymmrodorion: Session 1922-1923 (Supplemental Volume)*.
"Goronwy Owen (poet)." http://en.wikipedia.org.
"Goronwy Owen: 18th Century Welsh Poet." http://www.tourbrunswick.org.
"Goronwy Owen's 'Cywydd Hiraeth.'" http://www.llgc.org.uk.
Gray, Arthur. "Gronow Owen in America." *William and Mary Quarterly*, Second Series, Volume 11, No. 3 (July, 1931).
———. "Outline of Evidence Concerning Burial Place of Gronow Owen." *William and Mary Quarterly*, Second Series, Volume 8, No. 3 (July, 1928).
Greenslade, David. *Burning Down the Dosbarth*. Talybont, Wales: Y Lolfa, 1992.
Gruffydd, W. J., M. A. *Cywyddau Goronwy Owen with Introduction, Notes, and Vocabulary*. 1907. Book digitized by Google from the library of Harvard University and uploaded to the Internet Archive by user tpb.
Jarvis, Branwen. *Goronwy Owen*. University of Wales Press on behalf of the Welsh Arts Council, 1986.
Jones, Professor Emrys, FBA. A Concise History of the Society 1751-1951* (*Based on *The History of the Honourable Society of Cymmrodorion 1751-1951*, by R. T. Jenkins and Helen M. Ramage) *Y Cymmrodor* Vol. I.

Bibliography

Jones, John Gwilym. *Goronwy Owen's Virginian Adventure: His Life, Poetry, and Literary Opinions with a Translation of His Virginian Letters*. Williamsburg, Virginia: The Botetourt Bibliographical Society, 1969.

Jones, Rev. Robert, B. A. *The Poetical Works of the Rev. Goronwy Owen (Goronwy Ddu o Fon) with His Life and Correspondence, In Two Volumes*. London: Longmans, Green, & Co., 1876.

Le Nevez, Catherine et al. *The Rough Guide to Wales*. New York: Rough Guides, 2009.

"Monument to the Late Goronwy Owen, Poet and Rector, to Be Unveiled Here." Brunswick Times-Gazette 27 Feb. 1958: p. 1.

Morpurgo, J. E. *Their Majesties Royall Colledge: William and Mary in the Seventeenth and Eighteenth Centuries*. Copyright by The Endowment Association of The College of William and Mary of Virginia, Incorporated, 1976.

Morris, Jan. *A Writer's House in Wales*. Washington, D. C.: The National Geographic Society, 2002.

———. *The Matter of Wales: Epic Views of a Small Country*. Oxford: Oxford University Press, 1984.

Neale, Gay. *Brunswick County, Virginia: 1720-1975*. Printed by Whittet & Shepperson, Richmond, Virginia, 1975.

"Owen, Goronwy." http://wbo.llgc.org.uk.

Thomas, Ben Bowen. "Goronwy Owen and the College of William and Mary." *Cymmrodor*, XLIII, 19-36.

Thomas, Ben Bowen. "Goronwy Owen: Rector of St. Andrew's, Brunswick County, Virginia, 1760-69." *Cymmrodor*, XLIV, 113-25.

Tyler, Dr. Lyon G. "Goronwy Owen." *William and Mary College Quarterly* Volume 9, No. 3 (January, 1901).

Williams, Edwin T. "Goronwy Owen: A Welsh Bard in Virginia." *Virginia Cavalcade* Volume IX, Number 2 (Autumn, 1959): 42-47.

———. "The Flame That Will Never Die." *Brunswick Times-Gazette* June, 1957.

Williams, W. D. *Goronwy Owen*. Cardiff: University of Wales Press, 1951.

www.ingramcontent.com/pod-product-compliance
Lightning Source LLC
Chambersburg PA
CBHW060822190426
43197CB00038B/2181